SHRUBS AND TREES
FOR SMALL GARDENS

Small Garden Series

Editor: C. E. Lucas Phillips

SHRUBS AND TREES FOR SMALL GARDENS

CHRISTOPHER LLOYD

Revised edition

A PAN ORIGINAL

PAN BOOKS LTD : LONDON

First published 1965 by Pan Books Ltd,
33 Tothill Street, London, S.W.1

ISBN 0 330 23078 6

2nd (Revised) Printing 1972

© Christopher Lloyd 1965, 1972

Printed in Great Britain by
Richard Clay (The Chaucer Press), Ltd, Bungay, Suffolk

CONTENTS

ILLUSTRATIONS IN COLOUR

between pages 72 and 73

Camellia × williamsii 'Donation'
Fuchsia 'Mme Cornelissen'
Skimmia japonica
Kalmia latifolia
Acer griseum
Acer palmatum 'Atropurpureum'
Daphne odora 'Aureo-marginata'
Romneya coulteri

IN BLACK AND WHITE

between pages 48 and 49

Garrya elliptica
Wisteria sinensis
Viburnum tomentosum plicatum
Clematis Mme Baron-Veillard
Magnolia stellata
Griselinia littoralis hedge
Kerria japonica

between pages 96 and 97

Chamaecyparis lawsoniana Fletcheri
Rhododendron fastuosum plenum
Lupinus arboreus
Skimmia japonica
Pieris japonica variegata
Genista lydia

LINE DRAWINGS

EDITOR'S FOREWORD

I AM delighted that Mr Lloyd should be the author of the first book in this series designed specially for the smaller gardens of today. He is not only a highly trained horticulturist, but also, as his M.A. and B.Sc. degrees testify, combines the humanities with science. Thus his technical knowledge is imparted with a nice sense of English and a touch of native humour.

You can go and see his home and garden for yourself any day of the week, except Mondays, from May to September, and learn much thereby. He lives in a stunning fifteenth-century manor house, known as Great Dixter, at Northiam, not far from Rye, and there he has turned part of the gardens into a nursery.

What is a 'small garden'? The city magnate and his junior clerk will have different notions. Some of the trees and shrubs described in this book will be too big for the pocket-handkerchief plots of cities, but most are eligible for the average suburban garden and all, I dare say, for half an acre. Mr Lloyd helps to solve this problem by telling you the probable sizes the plants will attain and he gives you most valuable information on how to raise them yourself at minimum expense – which, coming from a nurseryman, I call highly altruistic.

C. E. LUCAS PHILLIPS.

CHAPTER I

THE BEGINNING

E VEN WITHIN the compass of a garden of no more than an acre, and very probably a great deal less, the choice of suitable trees and shrubs is bewilderingly large. They come in so many shapes and sizes and habits of growth, from those which creep along the ground and never hoist themselves more than an inch or two above it, to those which soar skywards like giant knitting needles. It would be easy to fill a garden with a rich assortment of these alone. Personally, I think that to rule out herbaceous plants, annuals, and alpines, is to deny oneself some of the greatest pleasures of gardening.

Still, a strong case can be made out for an all-shrub garden. Once established, it needs very little attention, and many shrubs are such good ground-coverers that weeds have little scope for raising their ugly heads. If you say that you don't want a no-trouble garden and that you enjoy the mental and physical effort of growing an exacting plant to perfection, I am with you. But our energy and resilience must inevitably fall off with the years, and anyway it has to be admitted, even by a rabid gardener like myself, that there may be other outdoor activities to claim part of our spare time. And you should never become a slave to your garden; to feel that its demands are exorbitant. Never take on more gardening than you can enjoy as a relaxation.

With shrubs and trees you are more likely to attain this ideal than any other way. And they will comprise the basic framework of your garden, whatever else it may contain. Deeper thought should be given to their choice and siting than to anything else because they will grow larger and hence be more

difficult to move successfully if you find that you put them in
the wrong place after all.

This book in large part aims to make easier the choosing of
trees and shrubs for a restricted area. Often the choice will
hinge on personal preference: my preference, in this case.
But that is no matter, for an author's views and preferences
are what distinguish his work from the next man's. It is natural
that I should want others to enjoy the trees and shrubs which
have given me most pleasure. On the other hand, few plants
(any more than people) are perfect, and I believe in always
mentioning their shortcomings too. To see them in the round,
complete with all their faults and virtues, is to understand them
properly and to get the most out of them.

The vexed old question of plant names has often come between the gardener and a worthy plant. Botanical names can
be daunting. Not always: *Viburnum fragrans*, for instance, is
an easily understood, descriptive sort of name which readily
sells the good shrub which owns it. But saddle a plant with a
name like *Perovskia atriplicifolia* and, no matter how good, it
starts with a millstone about its stalk. We can also call it
Russian Sage, which makes life easier, but then we may find
that it bears no relation to other sages and is not, in fact, a
sage at all; which is deceptive, because we may use it in a
sage-and-onion stuffing and get a pain, and unjustly blame
the Russians for it, only to discover that the plant does not
even hail from Russia.

All of which (and much else) brings us inevitably to the con-
clusion that order can be brought out of chaos only by using
the "lingua franca" of botanical dog-Latin, for the classifica-
tion of plants in a book. However, all the useful common
names will be given too. Look up "genus", "species", and
"var." in the Glossary, which gives definitions of other
gardening terms also. When, in the same section, paragraph,
or sentence, the name of a genus has to be repeated, the
repetition is done by using the initial letter only. Thus, in a
passage on *Berberis*, only the italic *B*. is used in repetitions.

CHAPTER II

THE ART OF CHOOSING
AND BUYING

WHAT TO plant? is a daunting question for the inexperienced gardener. To be taking on an old garden, however neglected or badly planted, will at least give you the advantage of some already established trees or shrubs which can be used as pegs on which to hang other material, but a new garden leaves all the mistakes to you. I remember a new Council House estate in a Kentish village where the owner opted for a labour-saving lay-out consisting entirely of heathers. The whole lot turned yellow and died within a few months, because he was gardening at the foot of the chalk downs.

What Will Your Soil Grow?

The first thing is to find out what will grow on your soil. Look around and take note of the sort of trees and shrubs which are flourishing in neighbouring gardens.

You must know whether the soil in your plot is acid, neutral, or alkaline. If acid or neutral, you can grow every kind of plant suited to your climate. But if alkaline, i.e. with a high lime content, you must forgo nearly all heathers, rhododendrons, azaleas, their numerous highly desirable relatives, and a number more besides. This sounds grim but it does, in fact, leave plenty, only you must be aware of what you're up against.

Pan Britannica put out a very cheap Soil Tester, available through any garden sundries shop or horticultural chemist. By following the simple instructions given, you can test the acidity (measured by what is known as the "pH" scale) of the soil in different parts of the garden: in different parts because, for instance, builders may have scattered mortar in some places in the course of building and, however long ago this happened, the soil in these spots will retain a high lime content and be unsuitable for certain shrubs. A reading of pH 7 means a neutral soil; higher is alkaline or limey, lower acid.

Never add lime except where vegetables are being grown. Someone will tell you that clematis love old mortar rubble and you will dutifully collect some from a derelict building. All to no purpose. Clematis and every other shrub will grow perfectly happily without the addition of lime and some day you will be cursed (or will curse yourself) for having made that clematis site untenable for growing, say, a camellia by its side.

What Will Endure Your Climate?

Another factor which will limit your choice of material is climate. Broadly speaking, the western half of the British Isles is mild and moist throughout the year, under the maritime influence of the Atlantic; the drier eastern half experiences greater extremes of heat and cold, under the influence of the neighbouring continent. The west will therefore succeed best with broad-leaved evergreens, which like it mild and moist, while the east will do better with deciduous shrubs such as the Judas tree, lilacs, and the flowering dogwoods, which need dry, ripening conditions in order to flower freely.

Wind is the greatest enemy in these islands. Unless you can provide adequate shelter from wind, many shrubs and trees will fail to get established. Along our coasts the winds blow even more furiously than elsewhere, while salt spray is an additional hazard, but all is not loss in such situations. If local shelter can be provided, a greater range of shrubs may be grown in coastal areas than anywhere else, for frost damage is minimal.

Frost is the other great enemy, and gardeners who choose to live in sheltered hollows where frost collects on clear, windless nights, are asking for trouble.

And so, when climatic conditions can vary greatly even within a distance of a few hundred yards, it is difficult to know whether we may call borderline shrubs hardy or tender. My own inclination is to be at once adventurous in my choice of shrubs and philosophical in my losses. To have enjoyed a beautiful plant for several years and then to lose it is surely better than never to have enjoyed it at all. However, I realize that many amateur gardeners regard the loss of a shrub with dismay. For them it will be wise to play safe and avoid disappointments and to make certain that whatever they buy will unquestionably survive the fiercest possible winters.

Collecting Ideas

The best quarry for ideas on what to grow is established gardens. Public gardens often contain well labelled shrub collections and specimen trees. Many private gardens are open at key times through the season when they expect to look their best. You can find out details about these through the local press; by getting the excellent annual publication *Historic Houses, Castles and Gardens* (which includes all National Trust properties) from Index Publishers Ltd, 69 Victoria St., London, SW1; or by consulting the pamphlets put out by charities, chief of which is the National Gardens Scheme, headquarters at 57 Lower Belgrave St., London, SW1.

Most big nurseries also contain permanent collections of shrubs. It is an enormous help to be able to see how trees and shrubs will look at maturity, for you can then visualize how they will fit into your garden setting.

It requires a good deal of experience to get the most out of plant catalogues, which have been described as mines of misinformation. There are exceptions, notably the Planter's Handbook put out by George Jackman and Son, Woking, Surrey. This is packed with useful hints.

The show bench can be similarly deceptive, unless your eye

is trained to be sceptical. At an early spring flower show, for instance, a stand full of blossoming shrubs will contain some which are indeed flowering at their natural time, but many more which have been forced and would not flower in the garden until a month or two later. Equally deceptive could be the exhibit, in an autumn show, which is loaded with berries, but has probably spent the past six weeks or more wrapped up in netting to save it from the birds.

Beauty Over a Long Period

It is easy to be carried away by the charms of a tree or shrub seen in the glory of its flowering. But always find out, before you fall for it, how long it flowers, and whether it will do anything more for you through the year. Does it colour up in autumn or carry berries? Is its foliage charming in itself? Has it coloured bark or a beautiful winter outline? If evergreen, will its foliage delight us through the seasons or look sooty or in other ways depressing?

If it can boast of no extra virtues and, in addition, flowers for only a week or so, as does much spring blossom, then it is certainly not a good enough rent-payer for a small garden.

Seeking Advice

If you have a new garden to plant, it will very often be wise to call in an independent expert to advise you on the original siting of trees and shrub borders. Tell him what you would like. If you have your own ideas for him to work on, the final result is far likelier to be satisfactory than if he has to work in a vacuum. The best gardens always bear the imprint of their owner's personality.

Often it will be to the nurseryman that you will go for advice. Now, the time when people are most garden-minded is when the rain clears off, the sun comes out and they feel the urge to get cracking. This is just the time when the nurseryman will himself be busiest with tasks of lining out, of propagation, potting, packing, and dispatching.

Don't waste his time more than you can possibly help. Deal with him in one of two ways. Either say: "I have here a list of shrubs I would like to grow. My soil is such-and-such, my exposure is an open south-west slope (or I'm in a frost hollow, or whatever); which of these can you supply and which of them are likely to be suitable?"

The other approach is to put yourself in his hands; to give him briefly the basic facts about your garden and then to accept his suggestions.

In fact, either provide the ideas yourself or else use the nurseryman's, but for pity's sake don't ask him for suggestions and then hang around in an agony of indecision while he is fretting to get on with his job.

Picking Your Specimens

It is not a good plan to make a practice of shopping for trees and shrubs in general markets or chain stores. I know it is tempting; the specimens are handy to cart off without further ado and at bargain prices. Too often the bargain turns out to be a figment. There is such a remoteness between grower and customer in sales of this kind that the former tends to feel a reduced sense of responsibility while the latter has an uphill task to get compensation.

The products of firms which specialize in growing for markets, especially plant supermarkets, should be of good quality. Frequently, however, the large shrubs you find in a general market are what the nurseryman has failed to sell hitherto and have now outgrown their places. But the retail nurseryman, dealing with his customers direct, is naturally anxious to keep on good terms with them, and to give satisfaction.

You can't always visit the nurseries you want to deal with; some transactions must inevitably be by mail. But the ideal will always be to visit a nursery in person and choose the actual specimens you want, collecting them later at an agreed time so that the trees' and shrubs' ordeal of being moved is reduced to a minimum. This course becomes more attractive from year to year, as freight charges increase.

Don't go for the largest specimens. This is the hardest doctrine to put over, because 99 gardeners out of 100 are wildly impatient. They want to see nice large shrubs in their gardens right from the outset. The point is that the moving of a large shrub usually causes a serious check to its growth, whereas the small specimen can be transferred with little damage to its roots and will get away to a flying start. Its growth will, indeed, quickly overtake the large shrub's since the latter will mope for years and perhaps never fully recover.

There are a few exceptions to this rule, notably rhododendrons, camellias, and hydrangeas. These have huge, fibrous root systems which can be lifted at any age (though with considerable effort) and without much damage, but you will have to pay the earth for large plants of them, and quite rightly. But *see* Appendix 1: Shrubs and Trees for Impatient Gardeners.

The well run, well stocked garden centre is a boon to the hurried gardener, especially the weekend gardener, for most of these centres remain open at the weekend. All shrubs here will be container-grown, and hence amenable to planting without a check at any season, including midsummer. The only point to watch out for here is that the plants have been growing for long enough in their containers to be thoroughly established – not just lifted from the open ground and plonked in the container ready for a quick sale before the plant has had time to put out distress signals.

Some trees and shrubs do not grow as well in containers as in the open ground. The garden-centre-conscious nurseryman may be inclined to drop any such lines, because they do not fit in with his system. Your choice will thus be limited, and if you want to remain an individual in your gardening, you will have to turn to the specialist producers some of the time.

CHAPTER III

PLANTING, TRANSPLANTING, AND GENERAL CARE

Drainage

VERY FEW trees or shrubs will tolerate bad drainage and waterlogged conditions. If your soil is of the stodgy kind on which water is apt to hang around, the first essential is to drain it.

Tile drains, i.e. short lengths of pipe (often concrete, nowadays) laid end to end, are much the most efficient and long lasting and a 3 in. diameter is right for most purposes. Don't lay them too deep or the water will never get down to them to drain away. On clay soils, 18 in. is quite deep enough. Lay them all at the same depth and so that they fall evenly towards their outlet, at the lowest point. A ditch or bank is ideal for this.

The pipes are laid on the hard bottom of the trench and then covered with coarse clinker, gravel, or shingle for the next foot; then topped up with soil. A single drain will cope with about 6 ft of ground on each side of it. If required to do a larger area, lead in lateral drains at 6 ft intervals, from either side, herringbone fashion.

Digging

It is better to treat a shrubbery as one cleanly cultivated unit than to plant the shrubs in a series of circles surrounded by turf. This is because grass is an exceedingly greedy competitor for nutrients. The shrub border will need digging over

one spit (10 in.) deep. Remove a trench 15 in. wide at the
starting end and barrow it to the end where you will finish.
Then throw each row of soil forward into the trench in front
of it, with a twist so that it lands upside down. The trench
you finish up with is filled with the soil you first took out.
Before you start you want to spread a generous layer of bulky
organic manure or humus on the surface, which will then get
turned in. This can be compost, farmyard manure, chicken
manure from a deep litter house, leaf mould, spent hops;
whatever you can get hold of. Even peat will vastly improve
the composition of the soil, although it has no nutritive value.

The ideal is to get your digging done in autumn so that frost
can break down the rough clods and planting can go forward
in the spring. In this case it will not matter how raw and inde-
composed is the manure you use. But if digging is to be
followed within a few weeks by planting, then the animal or
vegetable manure must be well rotted, or it will damage the
shrubs by direct contact with their roots.

Excavating

Now let us suppose that you are going to plant a specimen
tree or shrub in a lawn or in a piece of rough grass.

Make the circle, which is to be kept free of weeds and well
manured, a good big one, 4–6 ft across. (A tree such as the
false acacia or a shrub such as *Rhus cotinus*, which are apt to
grow too rank and sappy if well fed, need a circle only 3 ft
across.) Remove the turf and set it on one side. Next excavate
the first spit (of top soil) and make a heap of it.

Assuming that the sub-soil now revealed is pale and of un-
pleasing consistency, dig out the next spit and barrow it
away. Replace it, first with the turves, turned upside down,
then with good top-soil from another part of the garden,
mixing raw or decayed bulky organic manure and half a dozen
handfuls of bone meal in with this.

Finally replace the top spit, working in well decayed, bulky
organics and a similar dose of bone meal with this too.

All this extra-deep preparation is to allow for the fact that turf, even when kept well back, is still going to compete with your tree, and secondly that a tree, being a particularly long-term proposition, deserves a specially generous start in life.

Never dig a hole and then go away leaving it open. Either the exposed surfaces will get unduly dry or, far more probably, a shower of rain will make a large puddle, which obstinately hangs about until the next shower makes it worse. I personally like to do the whole business of preparing and planting in one go, in which case you must tread firmly on each layer of soil as you replace it, since you won't be leaving it to settle naturally.

Perennial Weeds

If the site on which you want to make a shrubbery is lousy with perennial weeds, in particular bindweed (convolvulus), ground elder, and couch, it will be wise to treat the area during the growing season with a wipe-out, non-selective weed-killer, and to plant only when its effect has worn off.

Sodium chlorate is admirable for this job. If watered on when the weeds are actively growing it will be far more effective than if they are dormant. After a few weeks you may find that a few weed patches are growing again; these can be given a second dose.

Six months after this, the ground will be safe for planting. I have got rid of patches of ground elder – the most obstinate of all weeds – in this simple way.

When to Plant

As is well known, autumn and spring are the two main planting seasons. The advantage of autumn planting is that a tree or shrub which gets settled in then is less vulnerable to spring droughts. Furthermore, every job which can be completed in autumn is one less to worry about in spring, when there is always a frantic rush.

The advantage of spring planting is that, whereas most shrubs are bone-hardy once established, they may turn up their toes if a hard winter follows immediately on planting. If you have any doubts whatever about the toughness of the plants you are about to buy, ask for spring delivery. But don't leave your ordering till spring; nurseries have very low stocks by then. Unless your water supply is so desperately short that you have to take a gamble on an autumn planting, always order magnolias, hydrangeas, and all evergreens for the spring. Most deciduous shrubs can safely be planted in autumn. In fact, they can go in at any convenient time during the winter, as long as the ground is not frozen.

The planting of *container-grown* shrubs in summer can be most successful. No damage to the roots is involved and so there is no check. The ground is warm and congenial. So long as adequate water can be provided, conditions are excellent for establishing young shrubs.

Spacing

It is a great pity to plant trees too closely. If we had the strength of mind to thin them out when they began to get in each other's way, all would be well but, of course, we never have.

Twenty-four feet should be the minimum allowed between trees of an average spreading habit like a cherry or the crab *Malus floribundus*. Eighteen feet will be right for a small tree like John Downie crab or an almond. Your trees are your main garden features and nothing should be allowed to impede their development as specimens. You can fill in the area between trees with shrubs to your heart's content, of course. Growing on a lower plane, the latter will be perfectly harmless.

In a shrubbery, allow 6 ft between shrubs which will eventually make big plants; 3 ft between those near the edge which seldom grow more than 3 or 4 ft tall. It looks less speckled if you don't plant all your shrubs as singletons. Plant two or three together of some of the smaller growing ones like caryopteris, perovskia, potentilla, and hardy fuchsias. Two feet apart will then be enough and they will grow into each other to form one unit.

If you follow these suggested spacings, you will think how empty the ground looks, immediately after planting. No matter. The gaps can be closed with temporary fillers such as annuals, bedding plants, and bits of herbaceous material given by friends who are re-planting their borders. The alternative, of planting your shrubs twice as thickly and then thinning them out two or three years later, is more expensive and less satisfactory. Unless you have somewhere to put the thinned shrubs, which is unlikely in a small garden, you will be reluctant to part with them and the same old problem of congestion will find no answer.

How to Plant

As soon as shrubs arrive from a nursery, unpack them. If the roots look at all dry, soak them for several hours in a bucket of water (or in a pond). You may not be ready to plant them where you want them, in which case plant them temporarily in a spare patch and water well.

Always examine a tree or shrub critically before planting it. Some of its roots are likely to be damaged; broken and torn roots do not heal at all well. With a sharp knife make a clean undercut above each wound, so that the cut surface faces downwards. A clean cut like this calluses over and heals much the quickest.

Next, examine the proportion of roots to shoots. There should be as much of the one as of the other. Nearly always, however, some of the roots will have got left behind at lifting. Those which remain will not be able to supply the top-growth adequately with water and nutrients. Therefore you should reduce the number of shoots forthwith.

The nurseryman will never have done this already, because he knows something of human nature: that the customer likes to see as much as possible for his money. If the shrub is of a kind which does not normally require pruning, just remove a number of the weakest looking branches, making your cut where each joins a stronger branch. Otherwise prune in the ordinary way, following the principles laid down in Chapter

IV. The same with deciduous trees, which will usually need pruning right at the start, whatever the condition of their roots.

Evergreens with damaged roots suffer most of all because, in every season, they are always losing moisture through their foliage, yet cannot replace it fast enough, thanks to the damage done. So their leaves shrivel. To prevent this, pick off half their foliage prior to planting – always the oldest leaves, which are the lowest on each shoot.

Trees and shrubs often fail to make a good start simply because of bad planting. But it is simple if you always obey the same set of rules. Make the hole to fit the roots, not the roots to fit the hole; i.e. dig a hole large enough to fit the roots spread out naturally and never try to cramp or twist them up into a hole that is too small.

When filling in, it is best to have a second person holding the tree or shrub at the correct level and in an upright position. No. 1 returns half the soil (well broken up) into the hole while No. 2 joggles the plant up and down to get the soil distributed all through its roots. No. 1 now stamps the soil down firmly with his heel, all round the specimen, then fills in the rest of the hole and stamps again.

At the end, the plant should be at the same level in the soil as it was growing in the nursery. You can always see a tide mark on its trunk or stems where the soil surface came. Too deep planting will result in rotting at the collar; too shallow leads to troubles from drought and from instability.

If the ground is very wet and sticky when you are planting, fill in around the roots with dry soil or with grit, and only firm the plant in gently. Otherwise the ground will crack on drying out and tear the roots apart.

Except in these exceptionally soggy conditions, always give a thorough watering after planting. Even when there is plenty of moisture in the soil this is a good practice, as it has the mechanical effect of washing soil particles into the air spaces, so that the roots are in contact with soil at every point, as they should be.

When you have to plant in dry weather, there is nothing to

get worried about. You then have to puddle your shrub in. Stand it in its hole and then fill up with water – this may require a gallon or two, but you can slosh it in as fast as it comes. Let this drain away and you will see that the roots are now all coated with a film of mud. Now fill in the hole, firming the ground vigorously in the usual way, and give a watering from the surface, but with a fine rose, so as not to pan the soil.

Transplanting

By picking the moment when conditions are just right and doing the job as swiftly as maybe, the transplanting of a shrub from A to B within one's own garden can often be accomplished without the patient realizing what goes on.

First prepare the new site and hole. If the ground is anything but sopping wet, give the shrub a thorough soaking six or eight hours before it is to be moved. Lift it with a spade; then, if any roots have to be damaged, they will get cut off cleanly. Using a fork, they will get torn.

Don't try to lever the plant out at the first bash of the spade. Dig it all round the shrub, under the extremities of its branches and well away from the trunk, without levering at all. Now go round the same slits again, levering gently and with an increasing tendency to scoop underneath the plant.

Finally get it out with as large a ball of roots and soil attached as you can manage, and straight into the new hole so that, again it is at the right level and, again, puddle in if at all dry.

Suppose, for some critical reason, you have to move some shrubs in summer. At this season, deciduous shrubs will be trickier than evergreens, since the formers' foliage is all of the softest and sappiest. Turn a hose on the shrub and soak its roots for several hours. Now cut each leafy shoot back by half. Strip all the remaining leaves off the entire shrub. Puddle it into its new site and syringe its naked branches with a fine-rose watering can as often as you think of it and always in the evening. Before long it will start unfolding new young foliage.

Staking

All trees need staking as soon as planted. Chestnut stakes are durable; their ends should be pointed and the bottom 3 ft tarred. There are various methods of staking. I dislike the diagonal type, as it gets in the way, and I consider the twin stake method unnecessary. My recommendation is to use a single stout stake knocked in on the prevailing windward side of the tree. There are some excellent long-lasting plastic or rubber tree ties on the market, e.g. Rainbow (plastic).

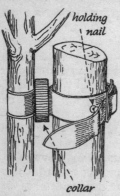

Fig. 1. 'Rainbow'
tree-tie

If you don't mind renewing your tying material each year, baler-twine (such as farmers use for baling straw and hay) is excellent because it is soft and non-injurious to the tree's bark. Many people use a harsher tying material and then protect the tree stem from abrasion with a collar of sacking. This is a bad practice, on the whole. The sacking keeps the tree bark underneath it in a saturated condition for months on end, allowing fungal and bacterial rotting to be set up, while a variety of pests are encouraged to roost in this safe retreat.

When the tree is a standard or half-standard, the tie is made at the highest point on the trunk before the branches start, so you want to make sure the stake is long enough to enable the tie to be made in the correct position.

Many shrubs also will need staking in their early years, no less than trees. If allowed to rock in the wind, a shrub will wear a smooth-sided hole in the ground around its base; this will fill up with water and finally kill the plant outright. Knock your stake in on the windward side, again. Tarred twine will be strong enough in most cases; otherwise use insulated (telephone) wire. Attach the string with a clove hitch to the stake and then pass the free end with a simple twist round each of the shrub's main branches in turn, returning to the stake at the end of the circuit with a reef knot.

Aftercare

Once your trees and shrubs are planted, the ground about them should be disturbed as little as possible. Some gardeners plunge about officiously with a fork and, when they feel the resistance of roots, are merely goaded into digging all the more furiously. It is easy to kill a magnolia stone dead in one such dig-over, while other shrubs will show their resentment in greater or lesser degree.

Surface mulching is the finest practice, using old leaves, bracken, peat, compost from the heap, farmyard manure, chicken deep-litter-house manure (rather sparingly, because it is very powerful) or lawn mowings, either fresh or rotted. The deeper the mulch, the more efficiently will it conserve moisture in the ground at all seasons. But never apply mulches to dry ground, as this prevents the penetration of rain through the top layer. Maintain a year-round mulch if you can.

If undecayed material, such as grass mowings or raw compost, are being applied during the growing season, add a general fertilizer such as National Growmore at 4 oz to the sq yd in spring, and again in June, but not later.

Weeds must be kept at bay, and for this purpose one of the modern pre-emergence weedkillers based on simazine will do the trick. Such are the brands obtainable direct from Herbon Ltd, Landford, Salisbury, Wilts., or through garden sundriesmen. An application made in February, before weeds start their new season of growth, will last for several months. But the shrubs *must* be well established before it will be safe to use these weedkillers.

Be very particular about keeping the circle around specimen trees and shrubs in turf, free of encroaching grass and weeds. Eventually the turf can be allowed to grow up to a tree trunk, but only after a period of six or eight years.

Watering

Scarcely a year passes without its dry spell between March and September, when your garden would benefit from irrigation. Shrubs and young trees suffer from drought much more than is generally supposed, and in particular the fibrous rooted ones like rhododendrons and camellias.

What is so deceptive about it all is that they may not show their need by any obvious signals at the time. After the really dry summer of 1959 there was tremendous mortality among shrubs, but death did not occur until the following winter or spring and was hence put down to various other causes. Even the usual sort of dry period lasting only a few weeks can have serious repercussions in the way of greatly reduced growth, and poor flowering in the following year. How freely your spring-flowering trees and shrubs are going to blossom is decided many months earlier, and one of the most important factors will be the water available to them at that critical period.

Mulches alone are not sufficient, and every self-respecting gardener should make arrangements for irrigating his plants. Now, a reasonable dose of water for a growing plant is *an inch in ten days*. (This figure should be doubled for wall plants, because the wall itself laps up half the moisture.) You can always find out roughly how much rain has fallen from the figures published in the local press. One inch of water is equivalent to $4\frac{1}{2}$ *gallons per sq yd*. So it is no bother to calculate how much needs making good for each ten-day period.

I hope it will strike the reader that if the whole of his garden is gasping for $4\frac{1}{2}$ gallons of water per sq. yd after a ten-day rainless spell, he very likely has reason to revise his scale of values on what constitutes a thorough watering.

The finer the droplets of water which your method of putting it on provides, the better it will soak in without caking the soil surface and running off. It is nonsense to think you should avoid watering your shrubs while the sun shines. I can think of only two shrubs on which I have known this to have a harmful effect by scorching their foliage: *Pieris forrestii* and *Hydrangea villosa*.

Certainly evening *is* the best time to water, because loss by evaporation will be at its lowest then and in the night, but it may often be more convenient to irrigate at some other time of the day.

Re-staking and Tying

Stakes are apt to snap off during a gale, which is just when they are most needed. Test them each year with a violent wrench to see how they are wearing. Likewise see to your ties, annually, and be sure never to let them cut into a branch. If girdled even with string in this way, a branch will be much reduced in vigour and may eventually die.

CHAPTER IV

PRUNING AND TRAINING

Shaping a Standard Tree

THE MOST popular flowering trees are bought as standards; i.e. they come to you with a ready-made trunk 5 to 7 ft long. Such is the case with almonds, cherries, crabs, thorns, laburnum, and mountain ash. They may also be had as half-standards, which are cheaper, and have a 3½–5 ft trunk; or as bushes, in which the trunk is less than 3½ ft. These are the cheapest, and can be the best form in some positions; for instance, when you want to see their blossom against the dark background of a hedge.

Few gardeners, on planting a young tree of this kind, give it any pruning treatment, but they should. The head of the tree, above the trunk, will be seen to consist of a number of wand-like, whippy branches. With the object of building up a stout, windproof branch system, these should be shortened back to within a few inches of the base of each, making the cut at an outward-pointing bud. A year later, repeat the procedure, cutting the new season's shoots back less severely this time, by about one third of their length. *See* Fig. 2.

Shoots arising from these main branches can either be left full length or, if growing into each other so that they cross and rub, cut right out.

The pruning described is best deferred till early spring on peaches, plums, and cherries, but can be carried out at planting or during any part of the dormant season on the others.

No subsequent pruning will be necessary except to prevent the crossing and consequent friction of branches. The less you cut plums, peaches, and cherries about the better, as the

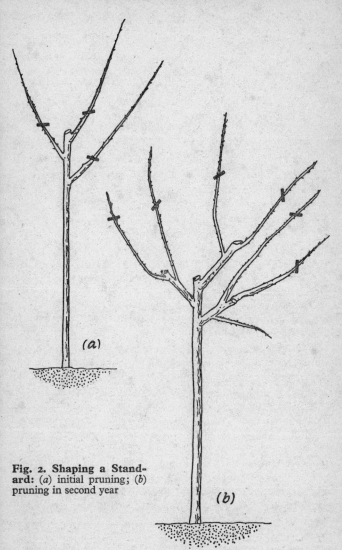

Fig. 2. Shaping a Standard: (a) initial pruning; (b) pruning in second year

wounds give entry to the bacterial and fungus diseases to which they are vulnerable.

Making a Trunk Where None Existed

Many subjects which you may want to grow in tree form will arrive as bushes branching at ground level. The work of developing a trunk, if you want the plant in that form, is all yours to do. Examples are the Judas tree (*Cercis*), the strawberry tree (*Arbutus*), the Indian bean tree (*Catalpa*), *Koelreuteria* and several of the larger magnolias.

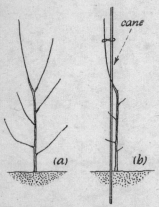

Decide first which branch or stem you will develop as the "leader" to form a trunk. No other branches must be allowed to compete in vigour with this. You can immediately reduce their vigour by shortening them. In the course of the ensuing growing season, this reduction can be continued, taking several bites at the cherry so as not to shock the plant. In the meantime, tie your selected leader to a stake or cane, so that it grows in the required vertical direction. By the end of the first year, your tree will be on one stem, with all its competitors eliminated.

Fig. 3. **Making a Trunk:** (*a*) the bush on arrival; (*b*) Leader selected and tied to a cane, its competitor eliminated, laterals reduced (and finally eliminated). Note cane driven well into the ground

Now, as this stem grows taller, first reduce by half and then cut right back to the trunk, the lowest laterals. In this way the length of clean trunk is gradually extended until it attains the required height. And there you are.

One possible subsequent danger is when a lateral, horizontally growing branch shows a tendency to become too strong and heavy. It should be shortened – not so as to leave a stump, but back to one of its own side-branches. Should the leader fork into two leaders at any time, be quick to spot the trouble before it has gone too far, and cut one of them out. A narrow-angled fork of this kind is always a source of subsequent trouble by splitting. Wide-angled branches are the strongest.

Tree-lopping

When a branch has to be removed, it should always be sawn off so that the scar is flush with the surface of the trunk or larger branch from which it sprang. This may entail more sawing and leave a larger scar than if you took the easy road of making your cut so as to leave a stump. Never leave stumps. They look hideous; they die, then rot and finally allow water to enter into the centre of the tree. If made correctly, the scar has the maximum chance of healing over. *See* Fig. 4.

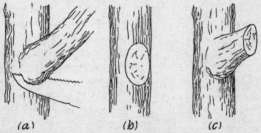

(a)   *(b)*   *(c)*

Fig. 4. Tree-lopping: First undercut the branch *(a)*; cut flush with the trunk or parent stem *(b)*; avoid leaving stump as in *(c)*

A pruning saw should be in every gardener's equipment. It should have an arched back and teeth on one side of the blade only. The other sort can do a fearful lot of damage if you are working in cramped conditions. To prevent the branch from tearing a slice of trunk away as it falls, start by making a half-inch undercut, before doing the main operation from above.

On a very large branch, even this precaution will not prevent some of the main tree fabric from being torn out. In this case, cut the branch off wherever it is easiest to do so, a foot or so from the base, leaving a stump. Then saw off the stump, making the cut in the proper place. In this way the weight of the falling branch causes a tear where it matters not at all.

After cutting off a branch, it is a good plan to pare round the edges of the scar with a sharp knife. The smooth surface this leaves will allow healing callus to develop as quickly as is possible. The wound should then be painted over with bituminous material, obtainable in proprietary brands such as 'Arbrex'. This rather soft, tarry substance is better than the unyielding white lead paint which is often used.

Shrubs

Many shrubs need no pruning at all. None of the evergreens do, except where it is simply a question of keeping them compact and within bounds, in which case a trim over immediately after flowering will meet their requirements. A great many of the slower-growing, deciduous shrubs need no regular pruning either: e.g. *Daphne mezereum*, *Magnolia stellata*, *Hamamelis mollis*, *Viburnum fragrans*, *Hibiscus syriacus*, *Corylopsis* species, most hydrangeas, azaleas, and lilacs.

It is a good practice, with these, to look into the centre of the shrub now and again, when the leaves are off, and cut out those branches which are dead or too weak to flower properly, so as to leave room for the development of strong young growth. But that is all.

The shrubs which really do need regular pruning are the fastest, untidiest growers. There are two main categories here: (1) those that flower in spring and early summer along the shoots which they grew in the previous year; (2) those that flower after midsummer and in autumn at the ends of shoots grown during the current year.

Group 1. Typical examples are the deutzias, philadelphus, weigelas, kolkwitzia, kerria, *Spiraea vanhouttei*, and *S. prunifolia.*

These can all be pruned immediately after flowering. The method is to cut out those shoots which have just flowered,

making each cut at that point where a new young shoot arises
or (if there are no such young shoots) at ground level. *See*
Fig. 6. Sometimes, when you are
too busy with other jobs, this
pruning gets deferred till winter.
The advantage of doing it when
the leaves are off is that you can
see the structure of the bush
more clearly. Young shoots are
unbranched and usually of
rather pale colouring. These are
left full length; *never* cut their
tips out, or you will materially
reduce flowering and make nonsense of the bush's shape. Old

Fig. 5. Prune back to a bud
within an inch of the base
of the previous season's
shoots

shoots which have flowered are dark in colour and have
numerous small side-shoots on which the flowers were borne.
If the proportion of young growth seems too small, it is either
because you have insufficiently pruned the shrub in the past,

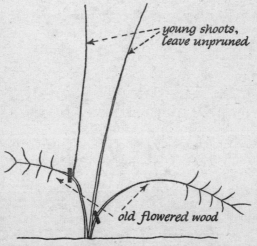

*young shoots,
leave unpruned*

old flowered wood

Fig. 6. Pruning a shrub such as Philadelphus

or because it is being starved and has not the energy to make the necessary growth.

Group 2. These shrubs flower from midsummer onwards on their young shoots. Typical examples are *Buddleia davidii* (the butterfly bush), fuchsias, caryopteris, perovskia, *Hypericum* 'Hidcote', *Spiraea* 'Anthony Waterer', the Canadian elder (*Sambucus*), *Tamarix pentandra*, and deciduous ceanothus.

To encourage them to make plenty of young shoots, the old ones that have flowered are shortened back annually. This is usually done immediately before growth is resumed in early spring, but if the shrub looks hideous or is in danger of being rocked by winter gales, it will do no harm to prune them at any time from early November onwards. If the shrubs are as large as you want them, cut back to a bud within an inch of the base of the previous season's shoots (see Fig. 5), but if you want to build up their bulk, reduce all shoots by only half their length.

CHAPTER V

PROPAGATION

I SUPPOSE it is the creativeness of plant propagation which makes it for me, and for many other gardeners, the most exciting and enjoyable of all garden operations. That it should be a closed book to (probably) more than half the gardening public is sad. It is simply a question of whether or not one has ever got into the way of it.

I don't believe anyone ever learned the arts of propagation just by reading. Demonstration and practice under supervision are what's wanted and there is, I think, a strong case for enabling the basic skills of propagation to be learnt by children at all schools. A utopian wish, perhaps. In the meantime it is a great help to visit the seasonal demonstrations of this and other garden operations given to their members by the Royal Horticultural Society and kindred bodies.

The chief methods of increasing shrubs and trees are:

from seed, by cuttings, layering or grafting.

Grafting (which includes bud-grafting, or budding) is great fun for the amateur enthusiast and for him I recommend *The Grafter's Handbook*, by R. J. Garner, published by Faber. By and large, however, grafting is for the expert and I shall not enter into details of method here. Brief mention should, perhaps, be made of the trees and shrubs which are commonly grafted, because then the gardener will be forewarned if suckers appear from the stock and will wrench them out betimes. The most familiar example occurs in roses, which are grafted on to various wild briar stocks.

Others include rhododendron hybrids grafted on the wild mauve-flowered *R. ponticum*; Mollis and Ghent azaleas on the yellow-flowered *Azalea pontica* (but plants from layers and cuttings are to be preferred); some viburnums such as *V. carlesii* on our native Wayfaring Tree, *V. lantana*; cherries on the wild cherry; plums, almonds, and peaches on various forms of wild plum; crabs on wild crab stocks; mountain ash and whitebeam either on their wild equivalents or on hawthorn (this is not so good).

Medlars are also grafted on hawthorn and so, of course, are the coloured and fruiting varieties of thorn. Lilacs are grafted on wild lilac or on privet; laburnums and brooms on wild laburnum seedlings, wisteria on wisteria seedlings (but these never give sucker trouble) and there are a number more, including many cultivated varieties of conifers.

Seed

The cheapest way to get a collection of new plants is from seed, and you need only to look through Messrs. Thompson & Morgan's (London Road, Ipswich) catalogue to see what a huge number of trees and shrubs may be propagated by this method. Some of them make large plants from seed in an amazingly short time, and you could easily stock your garden, gaining complete ground cover within three years, by sowing batches of the brooms (*Cytisus*, *Genista*, and *Spartium*), the cistuses and their lower growing cousins the helianthemums ("sun roses"), tree lupins, buddleias, tree mallows (*Lavatera olbia rosea*) and hypericums (St John's Wort). All would make a thoroughly lively display during their season.

They could gradually be added to or replaced (for the fastest growing shrubs tend to be the shortest lived) with seedlings of slower growing, but no less reliable species, such as daphnes, tree paeonies, lavender, spindle, magnolia, eucalyptus, and various conifers, to name but a very few.

But one must be aware of the pitfalls. Many tree and shrub seeds will take at least two years to germinate; paeonies, roses, cotoneasters, hellebores, and certain clematis among them. They may take up to four years and often they will not germinate at all.

Many more will not come true to their parent's name. The various species of maple (*Acer*), cotoneaster, rose, and berberis, for instance, are all madly promiscuous. They merrily cross and recross so that their offspring are likely to be the dimmest morons. Don't think that because you're sowing seed from *Buddleia* 'Royal Red', they will come any better than a slightly deeper shade of the wild mauve buddleia. And if you sow the variegated maple, *Acer negundo variegata*, or practically any variegated or specially coloured form of a tree or shrub, they will simply revert to the wild type from which they originated.

You must not expect too much even from the brooms. *Spartium junceum*, *Genista aethnensis*, *Cytisus albus*, and *C. battandierii* may come true for you, because they are species, but the hybrids will be so much mixed junk – pleasing enough, but nowhere near as good as named varieties, such as Burkwoodii, Moonlight, and Windlesham Ruby.

Seed Sowing. I recommend sowing all shrub and tree seeds in pots. Of course you can easily poke a thing like a conker or an acorn (scar *upwards*, please!) into the open ground and expect to get results, but even with these you have more control over squirrels, mice, cats, birds, dogs, and children (not to mention clumsy adults), by growing them on a special standing ground, wired in if necessary, and with the pots plunged to their rims in grit or ashes to stop them from drying out. If you stand your pots in a cold frame, you can control the amount of rain falling on them, which is a good thing to be able to do, but not essential.

Seeds which take more than a year to germinate usually need a period of freezing to break their dormancy, so don't think you are doing them a service by moving your pots to a frost-free spot in winter. Quite the reverse.

To sow: put a crock (which is a piece of broken flower-pot), hollow side down, over the hole in the bottom of a clay pot, better still, use a perforated zinc crock (available from Monro Horticultural Sundries Ltd, Waltham Cross, Herts.), as this

will prevent earthworms getting into the pot and blocking up
its drainage hole. Plastic pots need a handful of small pebbles
over their several drainage holes.

Next, drop in a dob of peat to serve as roughage, preventing
fine soil particles from washing down and, again, blocking the
drainage. Now fill up with compost; John Innes No. 1 will be
right for most seeds, but for very small ones (e.g. rhododendrons) use John Innes Seed compost (or the equivalent soil-
less compost).

Firm it down with the tips of your fingers (all eight of
them), but not your thumbs (which are too strong and uneven
in their pressure), round the perimeter of the pot. Flatten
out the surface. You can get a special circular pressing board
to do this, but the bottom of another pot will do. The level of
the soil surface should now be about an inch below the rim if
large seeds (e.g. paeony) are going in, but only a quarter-inch
below for fine seeds.

Now sow your seed finely, spacing those which are large
enough to handle individually, and pressing them in slightly,
so that they don't jump about and roll around at the next
stage, which is to cover with more compost. Then compress
again with the board or other flat surface. Generally speaking,
seeds should be covered with a depth of soil equivalent to
their own diameter; e.g. a paeony seed half an inch across
wants covering with half an inch of (compressed) compost.
Water from a fine-rose can.

There are slight modifications when very small seeds are
being sown. Before sowing, sieve some fine compost on to the
surface and press down, so as to get a fine seed bed. After
sowing, cover the seed with more of this sifted soil. Water
very carefully so that the surface is not disturbed and the seeds
washed around.

Cover the pot with a pane of glass and a sheet of brown
paper. This is to prevent evaporation so that watering needs
to be repeated only rarely, thus minimizing the danger of the
seeds all floating into one place. It is also to guard the seeds
from the danger of drying out (which easily happens, being
right on the surface) just as they are germinating. As soon as

they have germinated the paper must be removed. Very small seeds will either germinate within two or three months or not at all. It is the larger ones which may keep you waiting.

As soon as large enough to handle, pot the seedlings individually or else "prick out" into a seed box. Individual potting should always be practised in members of the pea family: laburnum, wisteria, brooms, Judas tree, acacia – as they resent root disturbance and should go into their permanent quarters as soon as possible.

Cuttings

This is the commonest method of increasing stocks of trees and shrubs. If the stock plant, from which the cutting material is chosen, is young and vigorous, the cuttings will root more quickly and make stronger plants than if taken from an old specimen which is no longer making much growth.

There are three main types of cuttings: "soft", "half-ripe", and "hardwood".

SOFT CUTTINGS

These are usually taken from the *growing tips* of young shoots, trimmed just below a "node" (see Fig. 7). May is the best month for many, e.g. hydrangeas, lemon-scented verbena (*Lippia*), fuchsias, *Senecio cineraria*, thereby producing a strong plant by the end of the growing season. Alternatively September is a good time, e.g. for hebes, bedding penstemons, fuchsias again and *Calceolaria integrifolia* – all of which are often hardy, but safest when overwintered in a cool greenhouse.

Some are most conveniently taken with a "heel" (see next section), peeling them off from the parent shrub when the young shoots are only an inch or two long in spring, e.g. caryopteris, perovskia, weigela, lilac.

It is simplest to trim the cuttings with a razor blade. Dip in hormone powder or solution, if you believe in it. The powder Seradix B is the most convenient to handle. My own experience has led me to give up what appears to me as just one more thing to do, without results to justify it.

Insert the cuttings with a dibber round the edge of a pot, as many as you like to each pot, making sure each cutting reaches the bottom of its hole. Use John Innes cutting compost which consists of 1 part (by bulk) of soil, 2 parts peat and three parts sand (actually $\frac{3}{16}$ horticultural grit – much coarser than any natural sand).

Being so soft, this sort of cutting is the most liable to wilt and should therefore be kept in a close frame and protected

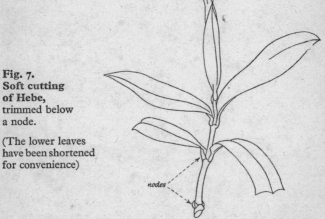

**Fig. 7.
Soft cutting
of Hebe,** trimmed below
a node.

(The lower leaves
have been shortened
for convenience)

nodes

from direct sunlight. Keep the foliage sprinkled by day, on a rising thermometer, but allow it to dry off from about 4 pm, as the temperature falls. If the foliage is wet by night, fungal rots are liable to set in. As a precaution against this, a weekly spraying with the fungicide captan is a great safeguard.

Woolly-leaved shrubs such as the senecios, *Phlomis fruticosa* (Jerusalem Sage), *Ballota* and the helichrysums, are so prone to rot that they should not be given airless conditions at all, but kept in a ventilated frame with shading.

As soon as rooting occurs, after two to four weeks, pot the plants individually in John Innes No. 2, return to a close frame (except as above) and allow ventilation after a week, thereafter quickly hardening the young plants off. However, this potting of autumn-struck cuttings should be deferred till the following spring.

If you have no facilities in the way of a frame for raising cuttings, each pot can be enclosed in a polythene bag, held in position by string or a rubber band round the top of the pot. Alternatively, put the cuttings into a clear glass (so that you can see what's happening) of water on a windowsill and, more often than not, they will make roots and can then be potted up or even planted straight out, if the weather is suitable.

This dodge is specially useful with shrubs of whose hardiness you are not too confident. You can take the cuttings in autumn, up to November; they will have rooted by the spring and, should the winter have been so severe that the parent plant has died, there you are with a replacement, ready-made.

The new Ward Propagator is first rate for small-scale work. It consists of a standard plastic seed tray over which fits a clear polystyrene cover and built into this are adjustable ventilators.

HALF-RIPE CUTTINGS

This type of cutting is always taken with a "heel". The shoots selected are young and very often are still making extension growth, but are beginning to get firm and a little woody towards the base. They are mostly in the right condition between the end of June and the end of September. Nearly all evergreens are included in this group and many deciduous shrubs such as roses, spiraeas, forsythias, buddleias.

Choose side-shoots of moderate vigour, of the current season's growth. Detach from the older branch off which they grew by pushing your thumb very

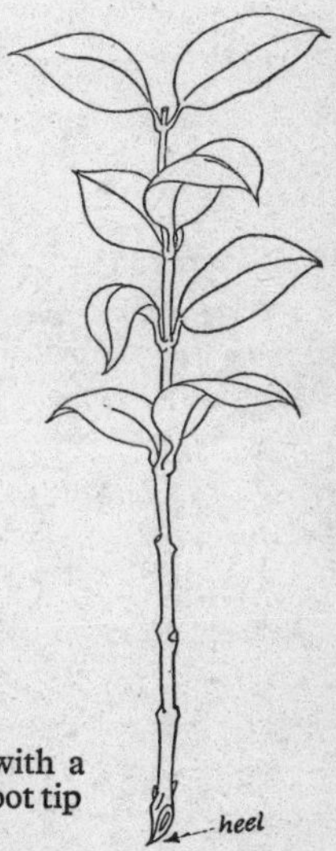

Fig. 8. Half-ripe cutting of Myrtle, taken with a small "heel". (The lower leaves and the soft shoot tip have been removed.)

heel

firmly into the inner angle of the shoot and branch, pressing your middle finger equally firmly on to the outer (obtuse) angle, and then levering gently outwards. The side-shoot will come away with quite a large piece of the parent branch attached. You now have a "heel" cutting. This must be trimmed, either with a sharp budding knife (a Saynor is the most reliable) or with a razor blade.

When trimmed, the heel at the base of the cutting should consist only of a very slight increase in the natural thickness of the side-shoot itself. The word "heel" tends to give an exaggerated idea of this feature. *See* Fig. 8.

The prepared cutting should seldom be more than 6 in. long, often less. If too long, and always if its tip is soft and growing, shorten it from the tip by cutting back to a node. Remove the leaves from the lower half of the cutting and take care, in doing so, not to leave any leaf-stalk stumps but not, on the other hand, to tear any rind off the stem. Treatment thereafter is the same as for soft cuttings.

HARDWOOD CUTTINGS

A stick, or even a trunk, of willow pushed into the ground will invariably take root and form a new plant. This is an extremely easy example of the hardwood cutting.

The material usually consists of foot-long shoots of the current season's growth, with or without a heel, prepared in late autumn or early winter after the foliage has dropped. It nearly always applies to the hardiest deciduous trees and shrubs. Although the percentage of success may not be high on the choicest shrubs, it is such a nice, easy method for the amateur that it is well worth setting aside a plot suitable for the purpose.

heel

Fig. 9. Hardwood cutting of Deutzia, taken with a "heel". (The spindly shoot tip has been removed.)

Examples of trees and shrubs that can be included are roses, mulberries, alders, elders, buddleias, spiraeas. The very easiest (e.g. willows, poplars, and the dogwoods with coloured bark) should be pushed straight into the ground on their permanent sites.

A plot for hardwood cuttings will be in the open, but must be protected both from cold winds and from hot sun. The ideal site is under a north wall which is itself protected from north winds. If the soil is naturally light and well drained, it needs no further preparation.

Drainage must be of the best and if the soil is heavy it should be excavated and replaced to a depth of 18 in. with a light mixture such as three parts grit, two parts peat, two parts soil, and stamped in firmly.

You can make individual holes for your cuttings with a stick or cane of suitable diameter. Push them in firmly, by $\frac{3}{4}$ of their length, so that the base of the cutting (cleanly trimmed with a knife to a node or with a heel) is hard up against the bottom of the hole.

The greatest danger with these cuttings is that they may be allowed to dry out in spring just as their leaf buds are expanding. They need a great deal of watering then, because they have not yet got any roots to help them search for moisture. By autumn they will be well rooted and can be moved.

Layers

The simplest way for a gardener to get an extra plant or two from any shrub whose branches can be pulled down to ground level, is by layering it.

Choose a reasonably supple and not too ancient branch. Work the part that is to go underground between your fingers and thumb so that it makes a gently crackling noise. You will be twisting it without breaking it. This makes it more supple and helps to check the sap flow, which is the big idea in layering. The point at which the flow is checked most sharply is where the roots will form.

Now make a slit hole in the ground and bend your layer into

it so as to make as sharp an angle at its lowest point as you
dare (often a right angle can be managed) without breaking
the stem. Again, you are checking the sap flow.

Keep the layer in the required position by pegging it down
at the point where it enters the ground. Tie the shoot, where it
emerges, to an upright stick. Firm it in with the whole weight
of your body behind your fists.

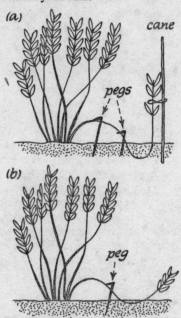

Fig. 10. Layering.
(*a*) correct; (*b*) incorrect

Layering can be done at any time of the year, but is most
easily practised on young shoots which are firm but not
brittle, between August and the following spring. The layer
may root abundantly enough to be detached and lifted in the
following autumn, but with hard-stemmed shrubs (e.g.
rhododendrons) it will most likely be advisable to leave it for
a further year and lift in the second autumn.

CHAPTER VI

CONIFERS

NEARLY ALL conifers are evergreen and nearly all hardy evergreen trees are conifers, so it at once becomes obvious that they are cut out to play an important role in gardens. Furthermore, many of them possess that invaluable attribute for the small garden in particular, of being slenderly tall. They will make columns ranging from 6 in. to 60 ft, and even the tallest may be no more than 6 ft across. Gardens lacking the advantage of sloping ground can still triumph over their flatness by exploiting these elegant spires.

But, of course, conifers include every other form imaginable, down to the prostrate ground coverers which never rise higher than 6 in. It is a fascinating clan. There are conifers suited to every soil and situation, providing the air is clean. But in the soot-laden atmosphere of large industrial towns, conifers are seldom appropriate. Even if their health can stand it, they look reproachfully grimy.

Those which are to be enjoyed as specimens should never be allowed to get crowded by over-close neighbours, or they will quickly spoil. If shaded, their growth tends to get scraggy and their foliage to lose its characteristic lustre. The beauty of many of the taller kinds depends on them remaining clothed with branches right down to ground level, but these lower members are, of course, the most likely to get too much shade, so one must watch out.

Most varieties of yew, cypress, and juniper can be propagated from cuttings, taken in a cold frame in early autumn, but they root slowly and are often none too easy. Seed, when it is set, germinates readily if sown as soon as ripe. However,

the majority of cultivated conifers are hybrids and therefore
the less likely to set seed and, if they do, it will probably not
come true. By and large, we should rely on the nurseries for
our conifers.

Abies. These are the firs. They bear the most beautiful and
often the largest cones of all, but are mainly forest trees.
Exceptionally, *A. koreana*, the Korean fir, takes many years to
make a small 15-ft tree. Compact and stiffly branching, with
the ½-in. leaves densely arranged all round the shoots, green
on top but conspicuously silver-grey underneath, deliciously
aromatic when bruised. Cones are borne like 2-in. candles on
the upper sides of branches, very freely even when quite young.
Before ripe they are a beautiful bluish purple with buff banding
where the scaly bracts stick out like tongues.

Chamaecyparis. False Cypress. Distinguished from the
true cypresses mainly by their tiny cones.

C. lawsoniana. Lawson's Cypress has many wildly differing
forms, of which the following is a small selection:

aurea 'Smithii'. The best golden cypress, where a tall
specimen is required, retaining its colour in winter better
than *lutea* or Stewartii. Only 10–12 ft wide at base when
50 ft tall. (Four Winds Nurseries.)

Ellwoodii. Popular variety, slowly making a neat solid 10 ft
column, clothed with small blue-green needle leaves.

Erecta viridis. Habit like the last, but its warm emerald-
green foliage makes a more cheerful impression in winter.
Run a sickle up its sides to trim them, from time to time. This
will prevent it from splaying outwards in later life.

Fletcheri. Most people's No. 1 choice for a dense column.
Neat, fan-like sprays of minute, glaucous needle-leaves.
Eventually reaches 30 ft × 10 ft at base. *See also* Chapter VIII.

Fraseri. Strongly vertical habit; a 12 ft, narrow column of
branchlets arranged in upright fans. Rich bottle-green.
(Sunningdale Nurseries.)

Stewartii. Graceful, pale yellow cone 40 ft × 12 ft, of loose,
feathery habit. Not so good as *aurea* 'Smithii' but more
widely distributed.

Wisselii. A splendid fastigiate specimen of only moderate

Garrya elliptica

Wisteria sinensis

Viburnum tomentosum plicatum

Clematis Mme Baron-Veillard on a north wall

Magnolia stellata

Griselinia littoralis hedge

Kerria japonica

vigour, growing to 30 ft × 8 ft in 40 years. Of stiff and chunky habit, the dark blue-green foliage arranged in dense tufts. Highly individual.

C. obtusa 'Crippsii'. An outstanding and brilliant gold-green variety of spreading, yet neat, habit. 18 ft × 12 ft.

C. pisifera squarrosa makes, in the course of many years, a huge silvery-green bush, 20 ft × 15 ft, clothed with softly spiky foliage. Most arresting. (Treasures.)

C. thyoides. White Cypress. An excellent, slow-growing tree for cold, wet positions. Dark green, slightly blue-tinted column, 30 ft × 12 ft, composed of minute scale-leaves. Masses of tiny brown cones. Nicely aromatic. (Reuthe; Hillier.)

Cupressocyparis leylandii. Leyland's Cypress. Might be considered too large and vigorous for the small garden, except that it is the answer to the impatient gardener's prayer, adding 2–4 ft to its stature annually. Broadly columnar, 12 ft across when 45 ft high. Plain green. A quick blotter-out of eyesores. *See also* Chapter VIII.

Cupressus sempervirens stricta. The Mediterranean cypress which gives so much of its romantic atmosphere to the Italian landscape and gardens. A slender, rich green column of ascending branches. Quite quick-growing. Not always considered too hardy, but hardy strains exist, and they survived the winter ordeal of 1963 unscathed.

Juniperus. The junipers are as variable in habit as the cypresses and are just as important to the gardener. Male and female flowers are usually borne on separate plants and the fruit is a dark blue berry-like structure used to flavour Holland-type gin (the word gin being a corruption of the Dutch for juniper).

J. chinensis. Chinese Juniper. A narrow column, 20 ft × 3 or 4 ft, of scaly green foliage, males being attractively speckled, in winter, with masses of yellowish blobs, which later bear the pollen. *Var. aurea* has the same habit and winter colouring but its young growth is yellow-tinted. This is the ideal kind of spire for many key positions in a garden design. (Reuthe.)

J. media pfizeriana requires a good deal of room but would usefully clothe a difficult bank of thin chalky soil. Up to 5 ft tall but very spreading. Pleasant green leaves, the branchlets drooping at their tips.

J. communis hibernica. The Irish form of our wild common juniper. Small, compact column of formal appearance, grey-green, up to 8 ft tall.

J. horizontalis. A creeping ground-coverer, no more than 6 in. high. Of bluish-green colouring, the tips of its young shoots changing to purple in winter. Copes well with banks or rough grass in any open situation.

J. sabina. The Savin. Another good bank-coverer up to 4 or 5 ft, rather in the style of *J. media pfizeriana.* Like all junipers, excellent on chalky soil. Dark green.

J. sabina cupressifolia. Low, creeping habit of *J. horizontalis,* but a bright emerald green, very cheerful and pretty in winter. Up to 1 ft tall. (Hillier.)

J. sabina tamariscifolia. First rate, lowish ground-coverer. Up to 3 ft tall, eventually, its branches of rich green, spiky foliage arranged in layers and ledges. Makes a handsome and unusual specimen feature in a lawn, where it should be allowed gradually to encroach on the grass. Absolutely weed-suppressing.

Libocedrus decurrens. Incense Cedar. It would be hard to exaggerate the fine qualities of this tree. Will make a column 60 ft tall in 35 years, remaining only 6 ft wide. Its colour is the most cheerful bay-green and its scale-like foliage is arranged in neat, fan-like fronds which are themselves grouped in a rosette formation, giving the tree a remarkable texture when viewed at a distance. Easily raised from seed.

Picea pungens, the Blue Colorado Spruce, is best known in two of its bluest forms, *glauca* and Kosteriana. Perfectly entrancing when babies, consisting largely of incredibly blue young shoots. Grows very slowly into a small tree. Rather disappointing in later life. (L. R. Russell; Treseder.)

Taxus. Yew. *See also* Chapter VIII. *T. baccata,* the common yew, is too large a tree for the small garden, but has many dwarf forms. *T. b. fastigiata* is the upright growing

Irish Yew. Dark and sombre, but dignified and often carrying heavy crops of its rosy-red berries. It has a number of yellow-leaved varieties of which 'Standishii' makes a very slow-growing, bright golden column. *T. b. semperaurea* is one of the brightest yellow, low, spreading, bushy types, 5 ft high by 15 ft across.

Keep Off!

Avoid the following conifers: *Araucaria*, the Monkey Puzzle, is fascinating when young, but never looks happy as a mature specimen unless its branches are allowed (and are healthy enough) to grow right down to the ground. It seldom has room enough to permit this. *Cedrus;* the true cedars all grow too large and forms of restricted habit lack charm. *Cryptomeria japonica elegans*, delightful and feathery in youth but unstable, heeling over with age. *Cupressus macrocarpa* (the common "macrocarpa"), this grows fast but dies even faster and is not hardy enough except on mild seaboards. *Picea abies* (also known as *P. excelsa* and *Abies excelsa*), which is the Christmas tree; dull when past its first youth. *Pinus ayachahuite:* magnificent $1\frac{1}{2}$ ft cones, but a difficult tree to keep healthy. *Thuja:* Thujas in general look like cypresses but are stuffier.

CHAPTER VII

TREES

(*See also* Chapter VI)

ACACIA (false). *See* Robinia.

ACER. Maple. Includes many admirable small trees. The Italian maple. *A. opalus* (Hillier), is gay with the pendant clusters of its bright yellow flowers in earliest spring, before the leaves; 30 ft high, round-topped. The ubiquitous green-and-white-variegated *A. negundo variegatum* is best treated as a shrub and cut hard back every other winter. Needs a dark background. Grown as a tree, its habit of reverting to plain green is difficult to control.

Several species are referred to as Snake-Bark Maples, because the bark on young wood (especially in its second year) is alluringly streaked and marbled white. Of pleasing winter appearance. Leaves colour well in autumn on suitable soils (not wet clay). In this group Acers *davidii, grosserii, hersii, pennsylvaticum,* and *rufinerve* are all good, the last having the additional merit of red leaf stalks and veins, all summer.

Japanese maples are included under *A. palmatum*. They need shelter from cutting winds in spring and from late frosts, but they usually sprout again if damaged. Difficult on thin, chalky soils. The varieties *septemlobum* and *osakasuki* have the most brilliant autumn colour, while *atropurpureum* has purple foliage throughout the season and colours up well, also. These slowly grow to 15 or 20 ft and make spreading specimens. *Dissectum atropurpureum,* a spreading shrub with very finely divided foliage, colouring briefly but brilliantly in autumn is included here for convenience.

A lawn group of three or five *A. griseum*, with 6 ft spacing, makes a beautiful feature. Slender tree to 20 ft, the small, trifoliate leaves colouring well; rufous bark on trunk and branches, peeling yearly to reveal an orange skin.

Almond. *See* Prunus.

Amelanchier laevis (*canadensis*), the Snowy Mespilus, a round-topped tree, 25 ft × 25 ft with quantities of spidery white blossom (akin to Prunus) for a few days in spring, followed by fiery tints in early October. Good lawn specimen.

Arbutus. One of the few, reasonably hardy evergreen trees apart from conifers, is *A. unedo*, the Strawberry Tree, native of west Ireland; hardy in south and west Britain. It is a 30 ft, round-headed tree with rust-brown bark and glossy, oval foliage and small white, urn-flowers in clusters in November. Strawberry-like fruits, tasteless but harmless.

Ash. *See* Fraxinus.

Bay. *See* Laurus.

Beech. *See* Fagus.

Betula. Birch. Birches are particularly hardy, thrive on the poorest soils, cast the lightest shade, never look heavy or over-leafy and have a delightfully twiggy winter outline. Roots greedily surface-feeding, however. *B. verrucosa* (*alba*, *pendula*) our native Silver Birch is hard to improve on with its white bark and naturally semi-weeping branches. To 50 ft, but slender. Its variety *dalecarlica* (*laciniata*), the Swedish Birch, is cut-leaved and makes a change.

Birch. *See* Betula.

Catalpa bignonioides, Indian Bean Tree. Rather large and spreading, 40 ft each way, but outstanding for its freedom of flowering in late summer with horse-chestnut-like, white sprays. Especially good in towns, benefiting from their extra heat and shelter. Hardy, but branches brittle. In the variety *aurea* the large, heart-leaves are yellow throughout the summer and the tree is less vigorous.

Cercis siliquastrum, the Judas Tree. Very distinguished specimen, its twigs and branches crowded with purplish-rose pea flowers in May, just before the round leaves expand.

Unusual and striking. Likes a hot spot; good town plant. Seed.

Cherry. *See* Prunus.

Cotoneaster. (*See* also Chapters X and XI.) Excellent small specimen trees, if trained and bought as standards, are made by C. 'Hybrida Pendula' and C. 'Watererii'. The former weeps to the ground, the latter grows 20 ft × 20 ft. Both semi-evergreen, laden with clustered red berries far into winter.

Crabs. *See* Malus.

Crataegus. The Thorns. Variants of our native hawthorn or may. *C. oxyacanthoides* may be had in white, pink, or red forms, double or single, but the best known of all is Coccinea Plena or Paul's Double Scarlet. Double mays hold their petals longest. Never likely to be overplanted, they grow into rugged, interestingly-shaped trees, 25 ft × 20 ft, billowing with blossom in May and June.

Other species of thorn of great interest are *C. crus-galli*, the Cockspur Thorn, with white flowers in June followed by orange autumn foliage mingled with clusters of large red haws, that hang on through most of winter, and *C. orientalis*, with deeply cut leaves, grey on the underside, large, clustered white flowers in June and big, coral-red haws.

Eucalyptus. *See* Chapter X.

Fagus. Beech, Cut-leaved, copper, purple, weeping, and common beeches all grow enormous, but *F. sylvatica fastigiata*, the Dawyk Beech, is narrowly columnar, 40 ft × 12 ft, clothed with foliage to the base.

Fraxinus. Ash. Too large, on the whole. Even the weeping ash, *F. excelsior pendula*, needs a lot of space, but makes a pleasant arbour on a lawn. *F. mariesii* reaches only 20 ft at most and foams with creamy white blossoms in June and bunches of purple seeds in late summer (Hillier).

Hawthorn. *See* Crataegus.

Judas Tree. *See* Cercis.

Koelreuteria paniculata, another of that rare and valuable clan, the late-summer-flowering tree, with small yellow blossoms in large panicles followed by seed pods like Chinese lanterns. Pinnate foliage, turning to pure yellow in autumn. 25 ft × 25 ft. Easy from seed.

Laburnum. 30 ft × 25 ft trees, whose yellow tresses show up best against evergreens, *not* against red, pink, or yellow brick. *L. alpinum* 'Vossii' has the longest racemes. Sets little seed and flowers regularly. Laburnums are quickly and easily raised from seed, but such trees will not have the longest tresses and will seed so heavily and exhaustingly as to flower only every other year.

Laurus nobilis, the Bay Laurel, used of old to crown the poets; nowadays to flavour rice puddings and stews. Tree or large, many-stemmed shrub 25 ft × 30 ft. A warm-toned evergreen of cheerful winter aspect. Ropes of scented yellow blossom in May. Can be clipped but nicest when free-growing. Gets severely cut in hard winters but sprouts afresh. Seed or cuttings.

Liquidambar styraciflua, the Sweet Gum, may get very big. Far more often only 30–40 ft and rather narrow. Maple-like foliage, changing (if you're lucky) to extraordinary purple, red, and orange autumn tints. Seed, but germination slow.

Magnolia. *See* Chapter XI.

Malus. Apples and Crabs. At one time included with Pyrus, and still sometimes so listed. All flowering crabs are grafted, but if you like to raise seedlings from pips of a purple-leaved, red-flowered variety, the chances are you will get something similar. Of these, Lemoinei is perhaps the best, being a round-topped tree, 25 ft × 30 ft with very large red flowers in May. Eleyi, Aldenhamensis, and Purpurea are almost as good. My own favourite crab is *M. floribunda,* a great cloud of many thousands of deep pink buds, opening to smallish pale pink blossoms. Its light green leaves and its flowers are darker in the variety atrosanguinea; some people prefer it. 20 ft × 30 ft.

A good, compact crab making excellent jelly is John Downie, 20 ft × 15 ft. Pale pink blossom, fading white. $1\frac{1}{2}$ in., oval fruits, a gleaming waxy red. Subject to scab in rural areas, and should be given the apple's normal pre- and post-blossom, anti-scab sprays with Captan or Lime Sulphur.

Maple. *See* Acer.

Mespilus. Medlar. One species, *M. germanica.* Large, solitary white flowers in June followed by quaint brown fruits with enormous "eyes". Cranks eat them raw when over-ripe or "bletted", and pretend to enjoy them. Pleasanter made into jelly, early November, before reaching bletted stage. Pretty lawn specimen, 15 ft × 15 ft. Grafted on hawthorn; should be worked low, so that the trunk is of medlar, not of thorn.

Morus. Mulberry. Never be palmed off with *M. alba,* the white mulberry, unless you grow silk-worms. A dull tree with worthless fruit. The black mulberry, *M. nigra,* is indeed handsome but scarce, expensive and mainly imported. (Hillier.) 30 ft × 40 ft, with branches naturally sweeping the ground, but these can be removed. Rugged, warm brown trunk and beautiful twiggy winter silhouette. Large, leathery, dark green heart-leaves. Succulent fruit, very tasty when dead ripe and almost black, but shared by wasps, flies, bluebottles, blackbirds, and starlings. Terrible mess under the tree, late July–October. Hardwood cuttings, but uncertain.

Mountain Ash. *See Sorbus aucuparia.*

Mulberry. *See* Morus.

Oak. *See* Quercus.

Peach. *See* Prunus.

Pear. *See* Pyrus.

Plum. *See* Prunus.

PRUNUS. A vast and the most important genus of small flowering trees, including the almonds, peaches, plums, and cherries. Think twice before planting any of them in bull-finch-infested, rural areas. These pests strip, not only the dormant flower buds, but also the leaf buds, so that twigs become quite naked apart from the terminal bud, which the bird can't conveniently reach. It is impossible to shape a tree decently in these circumstances.

ALMONDS AND PEACHES. (See also *P. tenella* and *P. triloba*, Chapter XI).

The almond, *P. amygdalus* (*communis*), with icing-sugar-pink flowers, is especially welcome for being out in March. A rather ungainly tree, 20 ft × 20 ft; needs careful siting against a dark green background.

Peaches flower only slightly later. Double-flowered types most effective. Aurora and Clara Mayer are both bright pink, Magnifica a rich carmine. Quite small trees, 12 ft × 15 ft. Liable to bacterial dieback; cut out all dead twigs. Peaches and almonds both subject to leaf-curl. Spray with lime sulphur when flower buds are showing pink.

FLOWERING PLUMS. (See also *P. cistena*, p. 66.)

The cherry plum or myrobolan, *P. cerasifera*, foams deliciously with small white blossoms, very early, sometimes late February. 25 ft × 25 ft. If young fruitlets escape late frosts, it crops well with red or yellow fruits, excellent when stewed. Its variety *atropurpurea* (*pissardii*) is much planted. Palest pink blossom; purple foliage. Charming, but seldom fruits.

FLOWERING CHERRIES

Although most commonly planted as standards, I strongly recommend buying these in bush form. The ugly lump which often develops where the graft is made, will then be unnoticed at ground level. In time, the bush will grow into a pleasant tree with several stems. Should you wish to pick blossom buds for the house, the branches will be far more easily reached.

This applies in particular to the invaluable winter cherry, *P. subhirtella autumnalis*, wreathed in small, double white (or pale pink in the form *rosea*) flowers, opening in any mild period from November to March, usually at its best early December. Budded branches force readily. 25 ft × 25 ft. A graceful, twiggy tree. *P. s. pendula*, the washy pink weeping form, flowers in early spring and must be grown as a standard or half-standard. Good lawn specimen, but *pendula rubra*, a richer pink, is preferable.

In complete contrast, the popular Amanogawa is of upright, lombardy-poplar habit, 25 ft tall, occupying very little space. Large, pale pink, almost single (or semi-double) flowers, mid-season. I personally dislike the stiff clumsiness of its branches, especially in mature specimens, and would prefer *P. hillierii* 'Spire', a slightly more vigorous and twiggier tree, some 8 ft wide at maturity, with single, soft pink flowers. Usually colours well in autumn.

One of its parents is *P. sargentii*, the best of all cherries for brilliant, early autumn colouring in orange and red shades. A well shaped, spreading tree 25 ft × 20 ft, flowering in earliest spring with bright pink single blossoms.

Of the typical Japanese Cherries (all varieties of *P. serrulata*), by far the most popular is Kanzan (or Sekiyama and, erroneously, Hisakura). Deep mauve-pink, fully double blossoms set among purple young foliage. Makes a great show, mid-season or lateish, but rather blatant in its usual urban or suburban setting. The tree's obliquely ascending branches look over-stiff until a specimen reaches maturity (after twenty years) and a more spreading habit.

Ichiyo (uniflora), a few days earlier-flowering, carries large, semi-double, disc-shaped blossoms, shell-pink (deeper in the bud) and hanging on long stalks among bronze-green foliage. Has great refinement and makes a beautiful, spreading specimen (Hillier, Marchant, John Scott).

Ukon (grandiflora) is the very pale yellow cherry most often seen. Flowers semi-double, mid-season attractively set among bronzed young leaves.

The Great White Cherry, Tai Haku, is outstanding in this class with huge, pure white, single blossoms, each 2 in. wide, among rich copper foliage, in striking contrast. Mid-season and a good do-er.

Okame is small enough for almost any garden. Deep rose-pink blossoms charmingly borne on a tree of shapely form and carriage. About 20 ft × 20 ft. Kursar is even better.

All cherries thrive better on a stiffish, moisture-retaining soil than on a light, arid one. They cast a heavy shade and have greedy, surface-feeding roots.

Pyrus. Pear. *P. salicifolia pendula*, the willow-leaved pear, makes an exquisite weeping specimen, 25 ft × 30 ft, with silver-grey foliage all the summer. Flowers and fruit of no significance.

Quercus. Oak. *Q. robur fastigiata*, the columnar form of our English oak, 40 ft × 15 ft, is a telling background feature of forceful architectural appearance. (Jackman, Hillier.) Young plants transplant best.

Robinia pseudacacia, the False Acacia, commonly known simply as acacia. Fast growing tree, 50 ft × 25 ft with deeply furrowed trunk and angular branches reminiscent of Chinese paintings. Light, fresh-looking pinnate foliage and laburnum-like racemes, 6 in. long, of white, fragrant blossoms. June. Very hardy but branches brittle. Therefore requires wind shelter and its trunk must never be allowed to fork. *See* Chapter V, p. 38. Seed.

Rowan. *See Sorbus aucuparia*.

Salix. The irresistibly pretty yellow-twigged weeping willow, so often planted in small gardens must be resisted at all costs, as it is far too rampant and vast growing. A pretty weeper of moderate growth is the purple-stemmed *S. purpurea pendula*. The upright habit and corkscrew branching of *S. matsudana tortuosa* have charm in every situation and in every season. Hardwood cuttings.

SORBUS. This genus includes the Whitebeams, which have plain oval leaves, and the Rowans or Mountain Ashes, which have feathered, ash-like foliage, but there are many intermediate forms. Excellent for small places.

A good whitebeam is *S. aria lutescens*. Its pale, greyish-white, unfolding foliage resembles magnolia blossom at a distance. White flowers and brownish-red fruits. 30 ft × 30 ft. *See also S. intermedia*, Chapter VIII.

S. aucuparia, the Mountain Ash, needs no description. The fruit ripens in August and is popular with birds, but they often ignore the yellow-berried *xanthocarpa*. 30 ft × 25 ft. There are several fastigiate forms, valuable where space is limited, e.g.

commixta, with brilliant red berries (Marchant, Hillier). *S. esserteauiana* carries small red berries in enormous clusters 6 in. across, and colours late, at the same time as its almost equally brilliant foliage. The habit and dainty glaucous green leaflets of *S. hupehensis* are particularly neat and its berries white, changing to pink, persistent and bird-proof. The foliage colours in autumn. To 15 ft.

Strawberry Tree. *See* Arbutus.

Whitebeam. *See Sorbus aria*.

Willow. *See* Salix.

CHAPTER VIII

HEDGES

THE ENGLISHMAN'S home is his castle, as we all know, and its walls are made of hedging plants. A hedge's main functions are to give shelter and privacy; to form a sombre backcloth against which bright colours will stand out the more effectively; to mask unsightly objects such as incinerators and cabbage patches; finally, to subdivide an area into compartments so as to provide a pleasant atmosphere of intimacy while also allowing changes of theme and an increased interest as fresh scenes are disclosed while progressing round the garden.

Some of these functions can equally well be fulfilled by informal plantings of mixed shrubs. However, clipped hedges take up less space and will be especially appropriate in a formal or semi-formal layout. Their advantages over walls is in lower cost and in not causing the turbulence which you get, particularly on its lee side, when winds batter a wall's unyielding surface. A hedge gives before the wind and also reduces much of its force in the maze of its interlacing branches.

The chief obstacle to successful hedge growing is its owner's impatience. The swiftest-growing materials are often not the most suitable. Privet, for instance, just because it is fast, is exceptionally greedy and impoverishes the neighbouring ground. It also gives a lot of trouble by needing to be clipped three times a year to keep it looking decent.

Another outcome of impatience is the excessively close planting of hedges which is commonly practised. Increase the widest spacing recommended by any nurseryman by one and a half, and you will be about right. So, if he says 18–24 in. make it 3 ft. He does not suggest close spacing merely in order to sell more plants. Rather is it because he knows that when a customer plants a hedge he so often wants it to *look* like a hedge, without any gaps between the plants, right from the start.

This is very short-sighted, because the crowding thus entailed and the competition between plant and plant, will lead to starvation at an early stage in the hedge's life.

A hasty and impatient gardener is also likely to skimp preparations of the site before hedge planting. And yet a slow character such as yew, will put on 6 or 9 in. of growth in a season if its needs have been seen to.

Preparing the site. Excavate a trench $2\frac{1}{2}$ ft deep and 3 ft wide. Set the top soil on one side of the trench, the sub-soil on the other. If the soil is heavy and drains badly, lay 3 in. drain pipes along the bottom and cover with 6 in. of rough material such as shingle. Where one side of the hedge abuts on a border where you propose to grow flowers or shrubs, you will be well advised to follow the example of my father when making such a hedge fifty years ago. He laid $2\frac{1}{2}$-ft wide sheets of galvanized iron along that side of the trench so as to prevent the hedge roots from being a nuisance, and I am still grateful for his forethought.

Now replace the sub-soil, mixing as much bulky organic matter with it as you can get: dung, compost, leaf mould, peat, spent hops, and the like. The same with the top spit, only here the organic matter must be well rotted. Include bone meal and dried blood.

Allow to settle for at least six weeks before planting. Most evergreen hedges are safest planted in spring – April – but you must be in a position to water thoroughly in periods of drought.

Buy the smallest grade of plant available, never anything more than 3 ft tall, or you may lose a high proportion of the plants. The rest will get rocked by the wind and have to be staked and will take a long while to settle down. James Smith offers excellent material at amazingly low prices.

Good maintenance. Keep the young hedge free of weeds or its bottom branches will spoil, and the great object with any formal hedge is that it shall be well furnished right down to ground level. To this end, the hedge should be trained with a batter, i.e. sloping inwards from base to summit. The bottom of the hedge will then receive its fair share of light. The sides should slope 2 to 4 in. inwards for every vertical foot.

To take an example: if you wanted a 7-ft tall yew hedge, it would probably measure 5 ft through at the base. Making a batter of 3 in. to the foot, the top will be 18 in. across, which would look very nice.

A rounded top is preferable to a flat one, both from the plant's point of view (especially following snowfall) and for appearances. Note the amount of lateral space which this sort of hedge requires. A plant of slighter build, like *Lonicera nitida*, should be used where the hedge must be narrower.

Start trimming the hedge's sides and top at an early age. It may not make so much bulk so quickly, but will become dense and, again, the bottom branches will be stimulated. To keep it in good health, a mature hedge requires its annual feed just as much as a young one. Bone meal, hoof-and-horn, and dried blood are all suitable.

We can now review and assess the various types of hedging materials available. For bottomless purses the scope is tremendous. We are far from adventurous in our patronage of shrubs for hedging, but most of us will be forced to buy whatever the nurseryman can supply at a reasonably reduced rate for quantity. Conversely, he cannot afford to grow in quantity varieties which might be suitable and would make a change, unless the public is prepared to support the unfamiliar. This is something of an *impasse*.

Evergreen Hedges

Yew gives the smartest, most dignified final product. Fairly slow, but grows at least 6 in. a year. From 2 ft bushes at planting, you can get a good hedge in eight years. No good in smoky areas. Yew Scale Insect may be a nuisance in drier south-eastern counties. This creature excretes honey-dew on which sooty moulds grow. Spray with 5 per cent tar oil distillate as used on fruit trees (Murphy's Mortegg) in March.

Holly is also very handsome and better in poor soils than yew, but I would rule it out for a reason never mentioned in gardening literature: i.e. the painful discomfort caused by its very slowly decaying fallen foliage while hand-weeding or planting within 20 yd of any ordinary holly. However, Jackman and James Smith supply a virtually prickle-free holly for hedging, called *Ilex polycarpa laevigata*, or J. C. van Thol.

Cypress, for speed, efficiency, and a pleasant effect, is deservedly popular, so long as you choose the right kinds. Leyland's Cypress (*Cupressocyparis leylandii, see also* Chapter VI) is fastest of all and highly wind-tolerant. Can be allowed at least 4 ft spacing. Green Hedger (Jackman) is excellent and a far more cheerful colour than the form of Lawson's Cypress called Allumii, of grim and grisly winter aspect, though with pretty blue young foliage in summer.

The fine feathery-leaved Fletcheri (*see* Chapter VI under *Chamaecyparis lawsoniana fletcheri*) looks very distinguished

The fine feathery-leaved Fletcherii (*see* Chapter VI under *Chamaecyparis lawsoniana fletcherii*) looks very distinguished in a hedge and is sometimes mixed with other varieties of cypress. Plumosa Aurea has golden foliage and can be used in the same way. Indeed, a hedge of mixed cypresses looks very handsome, although parts of it will grow faster than others. But this does not matter in the long run.

Thuja plicata (alias *lobbii*), is similar in appearance to cypress but coarser, and I would therefore give it the go-by.

Box is often mistakenly supposed to be of necessarily dwarf habit. There are many kinds, of varying vigour, and Handsworthensis (Smith) will make a good 6–8-ft hedge quite as quickly as yew. For a 3-ft hedge, use our native *Buxus sempervirens*, and for a mere 6–9-in. edging, *B.s. Suffruticosa* is suitable. Box is excellent on light or chalky soil and the plant wafts a fragrance which is dear to many people.

Privet, as already stated, is ultra-vigorous and greedy but cheap and smoke-tolerant. The species used is *Ligustrum ovalifolium*, which is not 100 per cent evergreen. Its variety *aureo-variegatum*, the golden privet, can be effectively mixed into a plain green hedge. Too overwhelming used in large chunks on its own.

Euonymus japonicus, with its glossy foliage, can look

pleasing, especially if a few plants of the golden-leaved form (*aureus*) are mixed in. Stands up excellently to seaside conditions, but so does *Griselinia littoralis,* which I would prefer and which is also perfectly hardy anywhere in the midlands and south, once established. Its pale, yellowish green, oval foliage looks fresh and young at every season. *Pittosporum tenuifolium* (alias *mayi*), is a lovely hedging plant near the milder coasts. You can earn pocket money by selling it to florists when giving a hedge its annual trim.

Lonicera must have shelter, too, or else it browns. *L. nitida* is neatest in its foliage, but *L. pileata yunnanensis* (*nitida fertilis*) is also good. Lonicera hedges often deteriorate from neglect and are never the same again. Can be grown to 6 ft, but must have sloping sides. Needs three trims annually.

Berberis offers us several choices of hedges that are both evergreen and flowering. Outstanding is *Berberis stenophylla,* because it can be kept neat without losing any blossom. Clip late May, immediately after flowering. Cascades of bright yellow. Spacing 3 ft; grows 6–8 ft tall but not fast. *B. darwinii,* a deeper orange, is not quite so vigorous and the leaves are more prickly.

Among evergreen **Escallonias** (*see also* Deciduous Flowering Hedges) the old, rosy-red *E. macrantha* is most reliable, but Crimson Spire is also excellent and attains a good height more rapidly. By trimming these, at whatever season, you are bound to lose much blossom, but August is best.

For **Lavender** *see* Chapter X.

Propagation of all the above plants can be effected with greater or less ease by inserting half-ripe cuttings in early autumn, in a cold frame. Box, privet, and lonicera are ultra-quick; yew, holly and berberis are slow. The cypresses come best with bottom heat in a mist propagator.

Deciduous Hedges

Hornbeam and **Beech** are always said to be as efficient as evergreens, because they hold their dead leaves through the winter. So they do, and a depressing sight and sound it makes. They need be clipped only once, in July, growth thereafter being negligible. Copper beech hedges are handsome, and especially after their annual trim, when the secondary young growth is almost pink and in striking contrast to the mature dark background. All three come from seed.

Hawthorn or **Quick** is generally considered a bit rough for a garden hedge. I fail to see why. It is extremely cheap, makes an impenetrable barrier and looks pleasant. So thick, too, that even in its winter nakedness it remains effective. Seed germinates after 18 months.

Especially good near the sea, but hardy anywhere, is our native **Sea Buckthorn** (*Hippophäe rhamnoides*). Tough, spiny and dense; silvery willow-like foliage and amber berries on female plants. Seed.

A beautiful, silvery-grey hedge with large, toothed leaves, can be made from the **Swedish Whitebeam** (*Sorbus intermedia*) available at a reduced price from James Smith. Very hardy and quite quick. Again, good near the sea.

Deciduous and Flowering

Most deciduous hedges from which a maximum of blossom is expected, will be fairly loose in habit and may take up a good deal of space. They will be used mainly for effect and not as backgrounds. Exceptionally, deciduous **Escallonias** with a fountain-like habit, grow into good thick barriers. Such are Donard Seedling (shell pink) Edinensis (deeper pink) and Langleyensis (red), which mix well. Can be pruned quite hard, late July, after their main blossoming. Pretty hardy but not 100 per cent. Hardwood cuttings *in situ*.

Prunus cistena, a plum with purple foliage and wands of white flowers, blossoms so early that it can be cut hard back immediately afterwards and make plenty of growth thereafter on which to flower in the following spring. Quite dwarf, 4–5 ft hedge.

Many **Roses** are suitable, choosing your varieties according to the vigour required. Those of rather gaunt habit, such as

Peace and Queen Elizabeth, will be best 2 ft apart in staggered rows, thus . · . · . · . . Among the Hybrid Musks, the sturdy habit of Penelope (buff pink), its far-reaching scent and freedom from disease, strongly recommend it.

Rugosa roses possess the same qualities: Frau Dagmar Hastrup (pink), Scabrosa (magenta), and Blanc Double de Coubert (white) have the same qualities and the first two carry crops of large, globular red hips. Height 5 ft. Space at 3 ft in single rows.

No garden should be without a Sweet Briar (*R. rubiginosa*), and a hedge devoted to it is wonderfully odorous; it smells of stewing apples, especially strong in muggy weather after rain. Height 7 ft. Spacing 3 ft. Single pink briar flowers and scarlet hips.

Zéphirine Drouhin is suitable for a really large hedge. Wonderfully scented, double shocking-pink flowers all summer. Height 7–8 ft. Spacing, 4 ft. Subject to mildew, and should be sprayed regularly with Karathane.

Fuchsia hedges composed of *F. magellanica riccartonii* in red and purple, are delightful. Height 4 ft if cut to ground level annually, but 6 ft if pruned only half back. July–November. Spacing, 3 ft. Mrs Popple is an excellent variety, with same colouring, but flowers twice as large. Height 3 ft. Space at 18 in. Cut down to ground annually in spring. Very hardy.

CHAPTER IX

RHODODENDRONS AND AZALEAS

Practically no rhododendron will tolerate lime, and so this chapter must be skipped by the unfortunate gardener who lives on chalk or limestone soil. Rhododendrons and azaleas can be grown on any other kind. They are at their best on the lighter soils, especially if these do not dry out too much. To this end it is always a great help to add peat and leaf mould when planting, and to give surface mulches of the same material plus old bracken, compost, or any other decaying vegetable matter. Applied when the ground is moist, in autumn or winter, this moisture will be retained throughout the dry spells. The addition of peat also helps to make heavy clay soils more congenial to the plants.

They all have a compact and densely fibrous root system, which is largely surface feeding. Hence the importance of mulches and the reason why many of them prefer to live beneath the light shade of deciduous trees, especially deep-rooting ones such as oaks, which will not compete for nutrients at the surface. But the toughest rhododendron hybrids, which we shall consider first, are perfectly happy in full sunlight, if need be. They, and azaleas also, can be moved at any age, with a huge ball of soil and roots, and at almost any season, but preferably between September and April. When planting, be careful not to bury the stem, for they are liable to collar rot (see Chapter III).

Botanically there is no distinction between rhododendrons and azaleas. Therefore, when I have to give a botanical name, it will always be Rhododendron (*R.*). However, we all think we know what we mean by an azalea, so I shall discuss this

group separately. Our subdivisions will therefore be as
follows:

 The Hardy Hybrids, or "Ironclads", or popular choice.
 Dwarf and Small-leaved Rhododendrons (all hybrids).
 Rhododendron species.
 Deciduous Azaleas.
 Evergreen or semi-evergreen azaleas (Kurumes *et al.*).

The 'Ironclads'

Here we have the large, laurel-leaved hybrids, many of
which make very big shrubs in time, but all may be pruned
severely into old wood, if necessary, for preference in late
winter. Some can be chosen for their dwarf, compact habit.
Their flowering season extends from Christmas till July and
they make a blaze of colour in their season. These rhododendrons are dense at all times, and a very good screen. Their
leaves are an uninteresting shape and can look depressing and
depressed, especially in frosty spells, when they hang limp
and curled up; or in towns, when soot-begrimed.

Commerical propagation of this group is often by grafting
on seedlings of *R. ponticum,* the common mauve rhododendron
which has colonized many hundreds of British acres from
Scotland to Sussex. As a rootstock, it often suckers. In one's
own garden any branches which reach to the ground are easily
layered. The following is a selection of twenty of the most
reliable:

Alice. Nicely shaped pink flowers of moderate size. May/
June. Tall.

Bagshot Ruby. Crimson with dark spot. Mid-season. Tall.

Betty Wormald. Deep pink, darkest at margins. Faint,
purple blotch. May/June. Tall.

Blue Peter. Frilled, lavender flowers. Dark blotch. May/
June. Compact.

Britannia. Bright red. May/June. Slow growing and
compact.

Cynthia. Carmine red with dark spots. Compact trusses. Early. Leaves hang forlornly in winter. Fairly tall.

Doncaster. Deep red with darker spots. Late. Low growing.

Eileen. Soft pink, deeper at margin. Very late (June/July). Medium vigour.

Fastuosum Plenum. Semi-double mauve. Mid-season. Medium height. Excellent old variety.

Goldsworth Yellow. The best in this colour. Apricot buds opening to primrose. May. Medium vigour.

Mme. de Bruin. Cerise red, very prolific. May/June. Fairly tall.

Mars. Deep, true red with white anthers. Late. Compact.

Nobleanum. Crimson and its white variety Album. Very early, sometimes at Christmas. Compact.

Pink Pearl. Large loose truss of enormous, voluptuous pink blossoms, fading. Mid-season, moderate vigour.

Purple Splendour. Tight truss of smallish, royal purple flowers with crimped margins. Late (June). Medium vigour.

Sappho. White, heavily spotted and blotched deep purple. Late. Tall.

Souvenir de Dr S. Endtz. Bright 'shocking' pink in large, loose trusses like Pink Pearl. May. Compact.

Starfish. Bright pink, especially at margins, with pointed lobes. Crimson spotted. May. Medium vigour.

Susan. Lavender. Early. Medium vigour.

Dwarf and Small-leaved Rhododendron Hybrids

Some of these come very near to being azaleas. All may be propagated from half-ripe cuttings.

Blue Diamond. Of softer colouring than the next, with larger flowers and more open habit. May.

Blue Tit. Dense bush, slowly to 3 ft or more. Masses of small, near-blue flowers. Very bright. May.

Lady Chamberlain. Delightful shrub to 6 ft with clusters of long, tubular flowers, usually salmon-apricot. Neat, rounded foliage, glaucous beneath. If you like this (heaven help you if you don't), try the nearly related and similar *cinnabarinum* (orange-red), **roylei** (dusky red), and **Lady Rosebery** (rosy red).

Rhododendron Species

The gardener who gets really interested in rhododendrons, will not be content to stop at the hybrids. The species include a fantastic variety of flower, leaf, and plant form. Many are not as easy as the well-tried hybrids, needing more protection from both wind and sun. They are propagated from seed, cuttings or layers (where the habit of the plant allows) and should never be grafted. Specialist nurseries in this field are Hillier, Reuthe, and Sunningdale. As a small sample you might try:

R. campylocarpum. 4–8 ft, with heart-shaped leaves, white beneath. Soft yellow, wide-open bells in May. Hardy anywhere if not unduly exposed.

R. haematodes. 3–4 ft, its laurel-shaped leaves densely brown-felted beneath. Brilliant scarlet-crimson flowers, May/June. Hardy.

R. leucaspis. Exquisite dwarf species to 2 ft. Young leaves bronze. Flowers pure white, 2 in. wide, opening flat with broadly overlapping segments. Brown anthers contrast strikingly. February–April. Needs protection from late frosts by proximity of other shrubs. A great favourite with the famous rhododendron-hunter, F. Kingdon-Ward. Seed.

R. macabeanum is just one suggestion among the fascinating group of very large-leaved rhododendrons with felted undersurfaces. Creamy or (in its best forms) rich yellow, wide-mouthed bells in showy clusters. April. If protected from wind and sun, and in a moist climate, becomes tree-like in time, but much lower growing in the east.

R. orbiculare has particularly attractive, smooth, rounded foliage, glaucous beneath. Compact shrub to 6 ft tall and broader. Wide bells of mauve-tinged rose colouring, April/May. Hardy.

R. thomsonii. 8-ft shrub with roundish heart-leaves, glaucous beneath. Sumptuous, blood-red, open-mouthed bells, 2½ in. wide, in March. Hardy and easy.

R. williamsianum. A gem of a shrub like a miniature *orbiculare*, 3 ft tall by 5 ft across. Compact with rounded foliage, bronze when young. Soft, pure rose bell-flowers, 2¼ in. wide. April. Needs wind protection and light shade.

Deciduous Azaleas

These mostly have large flowers in showy trusses. As regards parentage, they are tremendously mixed, but a few species are also well worth growing and shall be mentioned first. All need some protection from cutting winds. Layers and seeds are the usual methods of propagation.

R. luteum (*Azalea pontica*). Parent of the Ghent hybrids and, on to it they are often (but should not be) grafted. Large, spreading bush with yellow flowers and startling autumn colouring. Leaves and flowers have the strong, slightly putrid azalea scent which most people like. Makes a very fine hedge.

R. mucronulatum. Rather thin, spindly shrub to 6 ft, but set with bright rosy-purple flowers. December–February, frost permitting.

R. schlippenbachii. Large, soft pink flowers on 6 ft shrub. April/May. Protect from spring frosts. Orange, yellow, and crimson autumn colour.

R. vaseyi. Pale pink, speckled flowers, 6–8 ft. April/May. An easy one.

R. viscosum. One of the 'Swamp Honeysuckles' from N. America. Flowers small but numerous, heavily scented, very late; June/July. 6–8 ft. Ultra-hardy.

Of the hybrids, there are four main groups, all with flowers ranging typically from shades of cream through lemon, yellow, orange and salmon to the most scorching, fiery crimson, and flame. There is no point in mentioning the names of particular varieties; choose those of the colours you like best in the catalogues.

Camellia x williamsii 'Donation'

Fuchsia 'Mme Cornelissen'

Skimmia japonica

Kalmia latifolia

Acer griseum

Acer palmatum 'Atropurpureum'

Daphne odora 'Aureo-marginata'

Romneya coulteri

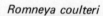

Ghent hybrids flower mainly late May and have the strong azalea scent. Single or double flowers.

Mollis hybrids flower a fortnight earlier and have no scent. Not as tall but somewhat larger flowers. More likely to catch spring frosts.

Knaphill azaleas combine the best qualities in the above two groups, with brilliant colours.

Exbury azaleas include the most varied assortment of colours and flower form of all. This strain is 'the latest thing' in azaleas. Named varieties are obtainable, or seedlings selected to colour, or mixed seedlings—in descending order of costliness.

Evergreen and Semi-evergreen Azaleas

Among these are the famous **Kurume** azaleas, planted to form spectacular masses of colour in the Devil's Punchbowl at Windsor Great Park. The fact that they are described as "evergreen" is no particular advantage, as they lose much of their foliage in cold winters. They need overhead protection from trees against frost and to prevent the sun bleaching their flowers too quickly. The flowers are small but so numerous that no part of the plant is visible, in the dumpier varieties. The taller kinds develop far more character in their plant habit.

Unfortunately the Kurumes are often a "sickly magenta or dirty puce" (Kingdon-Ward) but these colours can be avoided, if you dislike them. My suggestions would include **Alice**, salmon red; **Eddy,** orange-red; **John Cairns,** deep red; **Mikado,** orange-salmon, late flowering. These all derive from **Kaempferii,** which they resemble by growing 5 ft tall and being nicely shaped. For a clear pink, one cannot improve on **Hinomayo,** 4 ft. **Naomi** is a good salmon pink, late flowering. For a tall (4 ft) white, with a greenish eye, **Palestrina**; and for a lower, more spreading white with large flowers, the species **R. mucronatum** (*Azalea ledifolia alba*). This last is sweetly scented and can be grown in full sunshine. Half-ripe cuttings with a heel, late summer, in all cases.

CHAPTER X

EVERGREEN SHRUBS

(*See also:* Chapter VI, Conifers; Chapter IX, Rhododendrons
and Azaleas)

THIS IS probably the most popular shrub department. Everyone likes something to look at in winter. The advantages of evergreens are too obvious to need emphasizing. Their drawbacks are not so well appreciated. For one thing, most broad-leaved evergreens hail from warmer climates than our own. Consequently they are more liable to suffer from hard winters. Of those which survive this ordeal, many more lose a large part of their foliage or else have it browned in greater or lesser degree, so that from December till April, the fact of being evergreen imbues them rather with scarecrow qualities than fits them as objects to be looked at with pleasure.

So you do want to be rather critical and selective when making your choice, and not merely be guided by a marginal E against a catalogue description. The most effective evergreens in winter are those with a glossy leaf surface, such as choisya or camellia; and those with a warm yellow-green colouring, such as the bay and, again, the camellia. Some evergreens turn a purplish or bronzed hue in cold weather, and this, too, is attractive.

Ever-grey shrubs are at their best in the summer months, as a foil to other colours; they tend to look chilly and depressed under wintry skies. Most of them come from Mediterranean countries, and while they are well adapted to coping with wind, drought, and poor soils, they are vulnerable to low temperatures, especially when grown on heavy, wet ground.

They develop their palest colouring on rubbly, free-draining soils and are particularly good seaside plants.

Abelia. One hardy species, *A. grandiflora*. Loses much of its foliage in winter. Covered with very pale pink, almost white, tubular flowers, ½ in. long, from July till autumn. Not showy, but charming and useful. Prune by removing old branches, but leave the rest full length. Height 4 ft. Half-ripe cuttings.

Aralia. *See* Fatsia.

Berberis. Barberry. *See also* Chapters VIII and XI, and under Mahonia. The evergreen berberis are satisfactory shrubs without being wildly exciting. Handsome foliage, seldom shabby but usually prickly. A good, dense, spreading habit makes labour-saving plants of many. Thrive in all soils. No pruning needed. Propagation by half-ripe cuttings is very slow, but seedlings may give absolutely anything (*see* Chapter V).

B. linearifolia is the most beautiful in flower. Very rich orange, and showy. April. Slowly grows to 3 or 4 ft.

B. buxifolia nana, only 2 ft tall, but more spreading, could make a good edging hedge and is nicely prickle-free. Dark green foliage with purplish tints in winter. Yellow flowers in April, but not freely borne.

B. candidula is neatly dense, too. Makes a hummock 2 ft tall by more wide, the leaves' undersides pale, blue-grey. Horribly spiny. Bright yellow flowers in spring. Of similar habit but with more arching growth, making it especially suitable on a bank or retaining wall is

B. verruculosa, with long, slender, glossy foliage, silver beneath. Yellow flowers, May/June. Height 4–5 ft by more across.

In *B. gagnepainii* the leaves are up to 3 in. long with wavy margins. Bright yellow flowers in clusters, May/June, followed by black berries overlaid with a blue bloom. Compact to 5 ft and less spreading than many. Good hedger.

Broom. *See under* Cytisus, Genista, and Spartium, Chapter XI.

Calluna. *See* Heathers.

CAMELLIA. Perhaps the most beautiful of all hardy, evergreen flowering shrubs, after rhododendrons. Like these, they demand acid soil. However, camellias are excellent tub plants. Anyone with a lime-impregnated garden soil should grow them in this admirable way, starting with a rich, lime-free compost (John Innes No. 3 with flowers-of-sulphur substituted for chalk) and watering them with rain-water, never with hard tap-water.

Alternatively, brick in a trough against the side of your house, say 3 ft deep and 2–3 ft from front to back and 3 ft to 4 ft across. This will give the camellia more root room than a tub and enable it to grow larger. Add plenty of peat beforehand. Builders' rubble and cement can cause trouble when camellias are grown against a wall, and can make naturally acid soil alkaline.

If the shrub's foliage turns yellowish, water with iron sequestrine. The only other likely cause for yellowing foliage is too hot a position without a cool root run. Most camellias do not mind sun on their foliage, but they do demand a terrific water supply from April to September (*see* Chapter III), and especially in July while next year's flower buds are forming. Add liquid fertilizer to the water once weekly during the growing season.

Camellias are excellent in shade and particularly effective against a north wall. Always ask for spring delivery unless you can overwinter them under glass, following an autumn purchase. Although hardy once established, you can lose them when young, so protect them with polythene from searing winter winds during their early years and always give them a reasonably sheltered site. Never move house without taking your camellias with you. They are good movers at almost every season.

The forms of *C. japonica* are the most generally hardy, easy and useful. Beautiful glossy foliage, handsome at all seasons. The flowers are single, semi-double or fully double and rosette-shaped. The singles are exquisite (especially in white and red varieties) on account of their brush of yellow-tipped stamens. The semi-doubles can be a trifle unsatisfactory as the centre of the flower seems unable to make up its mind whether to be petals or stamens, and lands up somewhere between the two. Fully double camellias are very lovely in their way.

Confusion reigns as to their naming, and even a special naming committee set up by the Royal Horticultural Society has been stumped by many an old and well-tried variety. Choosing at the show bench is particularly successful with this tribe. The following might be selected:

Adolphe Audusson. Large, semi-double red. Upright habit. Mid-season.

Alba Simplex (White Swan). Single white. Early.

Appleblossom (Furoan). Large single, soft pink.

Arejishi. A large double red, the petals arranged informally. Early.

Donckelarii. Large, semi-double red with white streaks.

Elegans (Chandleri elegans). A popular, ultra-hardy bright pink double. Mid-season.

Jupiter. Medium, single red. Vigorous and erect.

Lady Clare. Enormous semi-double mid-pink; rather spreading.

Magnoliaeflora. Funnel-shaped flowers of medium size, semi-double, shell pink. This also has a white form, alba.

Mathotiana alba. Perfectly formal double white. Late. The pink form, rosea, is good too.

Mercury. Enormous blooms, 4 in. across, semi-double, rich red.

C. japonica has been crossed with the single pink C. saluenensis (itself a charming single pink of medium size) and the resultant race is known as Williamsii (in orthodox parlance Camellia × williamsii). Oldest and one of the best of these is the variety J. C. Williams, a tallish bush to 8 ft, of open habit with single pink blossoms in early spring. One of the more recent varieties of the Williamsii camellias is Donation, with huge double pink flowers in great profusion. Very exciting.

The flowering season of all these camellias depends very

much on the weather. In mild winters, many of them start in January, and they continue until well into May. The buds open in a prolonged succession, so that even if one flush is spoilt by frost, others will take over. The single flowered types such as Alba Simplex and J. C. Williams, tend to drop their spent blooms, which is a great advantage over those, especially the fully double ones, which hold on to them even when quite brown, so that one is forever picking the bushes over.

Most types can be propagated from half-ripe cuttings taken in July, preferably with bottom heat, though they will root in a perfectly cold frame after 10 months or so.

Castor Oil Plant. *See* Fatsia.

CEANOTHUS. *See also* Chapter XI. An invaluable clan on account of their pure blue flowers, tiny but abundant. The foliage is often neat, glossy, and comely. They grow fast, and are not particular as to soil, but must always be pot-grown and never shifted once planted out, as their roots are fleshy and brittle. Many make admirable wall shrubs and, being on the tender side, this is how they are mostly grown. An east or west aspect is usually as good as a south, and some have succeeded with them on sheltered north walls.

Plant all ceanothus in spring, as very young plants are most frost-susceptible; so are old plants of more than eight to ten years. Prune as little as possible but, where necessary in order to train to a wall, the best time on spring flowering varieties is immediately after flowering. Take half-ripe cuttings in September, from freely growing young plants.

Earliest to flower (March onwards) and easiest to train as a fan against a wall is *C. rigidus* with a smoke-like haze of rich indigo-purple blossom; delightful cotoneaster-like foliage, 8–10 ft. May is the season for *C. dentatus* in its various forms. The showiest is *floribundus,* with a sheet of powder-blue pouffs. Rather more refined and with nicer foliage, but ultra-vigorous to 15 ft and inclined to grow away from a wall is *russellianus,* a slightly deeper blue. *C. impressus* is the most attractive of the lot with tiny, crinkled foliage and a symphony in azure blue, May–June.

The variety Cascade resembles *russellianus* in its bushy habit; it is mid-blue and a wonderful sight in bloom. Where reasonably sheltered, it may be grown in an open border. So may Edinensis, with deeper blue flowers. These are May/June flowering. Autumnal Blue is inclined to flower at half-cock both spring and autumn, if left unpruned. It should be cut hard back each spring like *Buddleia davidii*, and then it concentrates its efforts on late summer and autumn; best in a sheltered border. 8–10 ft.

C. thyrsiflorus repens is semi-prostrate and ground-covering; no more than 2 ft tall, remarkably hardy and a strong sky blue.

Choisya ternata. "Mexican Orange." This is one of our handsomest evergreens. The leaves are polished, of a cheerful tone, interestingly shaped and pungently aromatic when bruised. The waxy white flowers are carried in abundance during May and waft a heavy perfume which reminds us that this shrub really is related to oranges and lemons. Often a scattering of blossom again in autumn. Wants a fairly sheltered spot and is best in partial shade, as on the north side of a house. Too much sun yellows the foliage. Branches damaged by cold winds can be cut back without fear. Height 6 ft × 8 ft across. Half-ripe cuttings in July.

Cistus. *See also* Halimium. In popular speech sometimes equivocally called "rock rose", a term also at times applied to the smaller growing, closely related helianthemum.

No cistus is bone-hardy in Britain but they are worth including in any but the coldest districts, being of rapid growth and perfectly happy on the poorest soils. They associate wonderfully with heathers and brooms. Mainly midsummer flowering, their blossoms are usually white but also pink and magenta. Their disc-like, fragile flowers have all the freshness of an oriental poppy, a huge crop unfolding each morning, and shattering in the early afternoon. The foliage of most cistuses wafts a delicious, spicy aroma in warm or muggy weather at any season, evoking the spirit of parched Mediterranean hillsides. Half-ripe cuttings in July.

C. corbariensis is one of the hardiest. A bold and compact

shrub, 4 ft × 6 ft, with neat, wavy-margined foliage becoming purplish in winter. Its pink buds in June contrast
prettily with the smallish white flowers, 1½ in. across. *C.
cyprius*, a rather loose shrub to 4 or 5 ft is outstandingly
gummy. The leaves turn the colour of oxidized lead in winter.
The large June blooms are 3–4 in. across, white with striking
maroon blotches at the base of the petals. *C. lusitanicus
decumbens* (sometimes incorrectly listed as *C. loretii*), is a fine,
low, spreading shrub, not more than 2 ft high, carrying its
flowers, which are white with red basal blotch, over a long
season from June to September. The aromatic *C. purpureus*
has large (3–4 in.), vivid magenta flowers at midsummer,
needing more shelter than the others. The soft colouring of
C. 'Silver Pink', is delightful but the bush is unduly scruffy
even in youth. All cistuses tend to get scrawny in old age and
should be replaced after 7 or 8 years.

Cotoneaster. *See also* Chapter VII and Chapter XI. A
valuable clan, though only occasionally thrilling. The habit
varies from ground-embracing crawlers to small trees. The
flowers are often inconspicuous, but the berries usually handsome and much appreciated by birds. Self-sown seedlings are
frequent, but may not be true to type. Half-ripe cuttings,
July–August, root well.

Starting with the lowest of the low, *C. dammeri radicans* is
absolutely prostrate, rooting itself as it goes. Excellent ground-,
rock- or manhole-coverer. Glossy green foliage; pretty white
flowers in June; coral red berries. *C. microphyllus*, again with
neat, glossy foliage, grows 3 ft high and then spreads outwards
indefinitely, but against a wall will run up to 10 ft without
support. Starred with white flowers, May/June. Berries pinky-
red, matt-surfaced. Of similar habit is *C. buxifolius vellaeus*
but with greyish foliage, for which it is mainly grown.

Of the taller kinds, some are really too large for the small
garden and scarcely worth the space. *C. franchetii* grows
rapidly to 10 ft. Loose habit with nice grey-green, oval foliage.
Small orange-red berries in handsome clusters. A good informal hedger where space allows; plant 3 ft apart. Rather
similar is *C. wardii*. The foliage and flowers of *C. lacteus* are a

little boring, but its large clusters of brilliant red fruits are spectacular, ripening late and hanging into the new year. 10–12 ft and also good against a wall or as a hedge.

Cotton Lavender. *See* Santolina.

Daboecia. *See* Heathers.

Daphne. *See also* Chapter XI. Discounting the small, rock garden species, the best and most reliable general-purpose evergreen daphne is *D. tangutica*. A compact, dark evergreen, 4 ft × 4 ft, with neat foliage. Clusters of scented flowers April/May and again later on young shoots, purple on the outside, white inside. Does not mind half shade but flowers most freely in full sun. Most easily raised from seed, but also from half-ripe cuttings.

D. retusa is similar but slower and not so large. *D. odora* is hardiest in its yellow-edged-leaf form, *aureo-marginata*, but should still be given shelter and full sun; flowers in terminal clusters, rosy purple outside, pinkish-white within, very powerfully scented. February/April. Height 3 ft. Easy from July cuttings with a heel.

Elaeagnus. The plain green *E. pungens* has a number of varieties, of which *maculata* (*aureo-variegata*) is, to my mind, the most beautiful of all evergreens in winter. Leaves elliptical, 3–4 in. long with polished surfaces. A more or less central area of daffodil-yellow is intermingled in streaks with several tones of bay-green. Wonderfully lively in winter sunshine and fine for cutting. Flowers produced on very old bushes only, in November; small and insignificant but richly fragrant. The bush is a slow starter but grows rapidly after the first few years, eventually 12 ft tall by more across. Branches frequently revert to plain green and these must be cut out. Pretty hardy but not 100 per cent. Half-ripe cuttings, August–September but rather slow-rooting.

Embothrium. One species, *E. coccineum*, the "Chilean Fire Bush". This spectacular shrub is hardiest in one of its narrow-leaved forms: *longifolium*, *lanceolatum* and Norquinco. These may be grown successfully on cool, acid soils in any but the coldest and most exposed districts. Tree to 40 ft in mild areas but usually they are large, suckering bushes to 20 ft. Clusters of brilliant red, tubular, honeysuckle-like flowers, May–June. Highly dramatic. Seed. Suckers.

Erica. *See* Heathers.

Escallonia. *See also* Chapter VIII. Those already mentioned for hedging will flower freely and continuously from June to autumn when grown as large, unpruned bushes, 8 ft high by 12 ft wide. Similar to them are the good old red variety, C. F. Ball, and Iveyi, a particularly handsome, rather stiff bush with substantial terminal trusses of white bell-flowers. An occasional hard pruning in spring will prevent them from outgrowing their allotted space, but at the expense of that year's blossom.

Of quite restricted habit is the stiff-growing, 4 ft Apple Blossom; well named for its pale and dark pink colouring, and a sheet of blossom for 10 days in June. But the bush is angular and scraggy, the flowering season far too short. Peach Blossom is similar.

Escallonias are not out-and-out hardy. Happiest near the sea but good inland, too. Half-ripe cuttings in July.

Eucalyptus. The Gum Trees from Australasia. They grow at an astonishing speed, but few are sufficiently hardy for general planting. Remarkable for the foliage of juvenile plants being often entirely different from and much more ornamental than the adult, willow-like foliage. If pruned regularly as 10–12-ft shrubs, the juvenile form of leaf is retained. Very nice against a sunny wall especially in colder districts. Prunings can be used in flower arrangements and last many weeks in water. One of the best for this purpose is *E. perriniana*, in which the juvenile leaf is circular and disc-shaped, tightly clasping the stem all round. Very glaucous, as is usual in this tribe. Moderately hardy, but succumbed widely in 1963.

E. gunnii is hardier and also suitable. Smaller, heart-shaped juvenile foliage. Can make a handsome 50 ft tree if sheltered, but liable to blow over. If a young plant is cut back to ground level after its first year and one shoot selected, thereafter, to form a trunk, it becomes quite stable. Better still: plant seedlings out when very young and before they get pot-bound. Seed.

Eucryphia. Except that young plants can succumb to a very hard winter involving more than 20 degrees (F) of frost, E. 'Nymansay' is an ideal shrub or small tree for our purpose, though rather slow. Slenderly columnar to 15 or 20 ft, only 3 ft across. Invaluable in being covered regularly with blossom in August. Flowers 2½ in. wide with four, broad, overlapping petals and a mass of stamens, tipped with reddish anthers. Sweetly scented and popular with bees. Tolerant of chalk, unlike most eucryphias. Likes a sunny, not too exposed position. Half-ripe cuttings; rather slow-rooting.

Euonymus. *See also* Chapter VIII and Chapter XI. *E. radicans variegatus* (*alias* Silver Queen) is a good ground coverer in sun or quite deep shade, 15 in. high, of creeping habit, and having green-and-white-variegated leaves with pink tints in winter. Will also climb a wall to 20 ft. Self supporting. Division.

Euphorbia. Spurge. *E. wulfenii* is boldly architectural, with deep green, somewhat glaucous foliage and great columns of pale yellow-green 'flowers' (bracts, really), April to June. 3½ ft × 5 ft; apt to sprawl. Cut old flowering shoots right out as soon as they become unsightly. Is generally hardy, but was largely wiped out in the winter of 1963. *E. characias* is very similar but slightly smaller. Flowers greener, with brown central dot. Seed; cuttings. A first rate ground-coverer, spreading slowly by suckers, is *E. robbiae*, 1 ft tall, very neat. Shade loving. Green flowers in April. Division or soft cuttings.

Euryops evansii, a most attractive little 1½–2 ft shrub with narrow, glaucous-grey foliage, toothed at the tips, borne in compact spikelets. Yellow daisy-type flowers in summer. Half-ripe cuttings, summer–autumn (Ingwersen, Drake).

Fatsia japonica (*Aralia sieboldii*), commonly but erroneously called Castor Oil Plant. The largest leaved and most exotic looking of all hardy evergreens. Shrub usually 6 ft tall, but can be 10–12 ft. Leaves 15 in. across, hand-like with seven fingers, a glossy and cheerful green. Flowers insignificant but curious, in globular clusters like those of ivy but white, November. Good shade plant. Shelter protects the foliage from wind damage. Seed or cuttings of firm shoots.

The variegated form is telling, splashed white near the tip of each segment. Cuttings only, come true.

Garrya elliptica, a bushy, quick growing evergreen with dark, oval leaves, is valuable for its clusters of 6-in.-long, pale green catkins, January/February. Grows to 8 ft or more. Usually treated as a wall shrub; good in any aspect, but can also be free-standing. Must be reasonably sheltered. Leaves brown badly in severe winters. Half-ripe cuttings July–September.

Griselinia. *See* Chapter VIII.

Halimium. This is the yellow-flowered equivalent of Cistus (though occasionally white). It likes hot, dry positions but may even then be killed in severe winters. Perhaps the best is *H. lasianthum formosum*. A sprawling shrub, 2–3 ft tall but more across. Small, grey leaves. Flowers 1½ in. across, bright yellow with a maroon blotch at the base of each petal. Mid-summer. *H. ocymoides* is good too, and very similar. Half-ripe cuttings in July.

HEATHERS. These comprise the genera Calluna, Daboecia, and Erica, with their numerous species and varieties.

The outstanding quality in heathers is that they are so labour-saving. Once they have covered the ground, weeds cease to be a problem. Furthermore, they have two tremendously long flowering seasons: from mid-winter to April, and from June to October. Their charm is of an informal kind, and they are best kept away from bricks and mortar. Though valuable in rock gardens and at the front of mixed borders, they look even more at home in informally shaped beds on their own, in a lawn setting.

You are specifically warned that, with four exceptions, all heathers need an acid soil; the exceptions are the *Erica* species *carnea, mediterranea, darleyensis,* and *terminalis*. It is no good attempting the others in lime-laden soils. Heathers are also sun-lovers, by and large, though *E. carnea* will stand a good bit of shade – it grows among trees in its native Alps – and so will the tree heath, *E. arborea alpina*. But the others tend to get leggy if shaded.

When preparing a heath bed, dig in as much peat as you can

afford and work peat in among the roots when planting. Leaf mould is excellent, too. Groups of one variety should always be the rule. Where the size of the planting allows, it is a good plan to have alternating groups of winter/spring and summer/ autumn-flowering varieties. Even on a flat site, undulations can be obtained by choosing varieties according to their height.

A rather close planting is advisable, so as to obtain quick ground coverage, but you must be rid of perennial weeds before you start. Low-growing heaths, reaching a height of up to 18 in. (and this includes the majority), want spacing at about 12–15 in. The larger tree heaths can be allowed 2 ft, or may even be treated as singletons.

Heathers must be planted firmly, and about $\frac{1}{2}$ in. deeper than they were in the nursery. If propagation is your aim, plant 4 in. deeper, and new roots will form from the buried stems. Lift a year later and divide. This works best on fairly large plants. The other method of increase is by half-ripe cuttings, July/August, peeled off with a heel, which needs no trimming. *E. carnea* hybrids root most easily, but, under mist, none are difficult. Layering is also feasible.

The only attention required by established heathers is an annual clip over of the summer/autumn-flowering group, so as to dead-head and keep them neat.

WINTER AND SPRING HEATHERS

Erica carnea, 9–12 in. high, flowers January/April. Of this type, King George is strong growing, carmine; Vivelli, not so strong, very deep red, with bronzed foliage in winter; Springwood White has particularly long and elegant trusses, very pure with fresh green foliage, and now we have Springwood Pink, with the same prostrate habit. These are ultra-tough.

E. mediterranea, with smaller pink flowers, grows to 4 ft, but can be severely cut in a hard winter. March–May flowering. Crossed with *E. carnea*, it has given the excellent hardy *E. darleyensis* (hybrida), $1\frac{1}{2}$–2ft, bushy and compact, soft purple, flowering November–April. It has a white form called Silberschmelze (or Silver Beads), while the vigorous Jack

H. Brummage has yellow foliage becoming reddish in winter.

If you can bear to take a risk with the weather, do grow the tree heath *E. arborea alpina*; it is pretty hardy, 5–8 ft tall, with feathery, bright green foliage, smothered in tiny white blossoms in April and May, wonderfully honey-scented and loud with humming bees. The pink equivalent is *E. australis*, but not quite so hardy.

SUMMER AND AUTUMN HEATHERS

Our most typical and widely distributed bell-heather, with magenta flowers, is the wild *E. cinerea*. Its variety C. D. Eason is particularly vivid, only 9 in. tall; Apple Blossom is soft pink, while C. G. Best carries fine, long pink trusses. There is a white form, *alba*, and a double white, *alba plena*.

The indigenous Cross-leaved Heath, *E. tetralix*, with soft pink flowers, grows naturally in boggy places, which affords a useful clue to gardeners. The foliage is greyish and this is much emphasized in the pale and hoary-leaved variety *mollis*, with white flowers. Con Underwood is a good carmine shade, with greyish foliage.

A natural hybrid between *E. tetralix* and the Dorset Heath, *E. ciliaris* has given us H. Maxwell, with a good upright habit, 12–18 in. high, and large, bright pink bells in substantial clusters.

The Cornish Heath, *E. vagans*, is pretty tough but not quite so hardy as those mentioned so far. Its flowers are borne in broad, spire-like spikes. These are 9 in. long in Mrs D. F. Maxwell, deep cerise, on a 1½-ft bush. St Keverne is a somewhat paler shade, while Lyonesse is pure white with conspicuously protruding brown anthers. Grandiflora is pale pink and rather late flowering, September–November.

The only summer/autumn-flowering tree heath is *E. terminalis* (stricta), the Corsican Heath, 6 ft tall with pink flowers in terminal clusters. Lime-tolerant.

Daboecia cantabrica (*Menziesia polifolia*), St Dabeoc's Heath from Ireland, makes a low (18 in.) sprawling shrub studded with rather large magenta bells over a long period. It has a white form, *alba*, and another called Praegerae, of a particularly fetching salmon-rose colour.

Last but not least our native Ling, *Calluna vulgaris*, source of heather honey and notoriously lucky in its white form. Particularly striking are the double forms, in which the flowers resemble beads. Elsie Purnell and the deeper Cramond are two modern pink varieties with *alba plena* a compact double white. Principally for their coloured foliage you should grow Robert Chapman, greeny yellow in summer changing to orange-red in winter and purplish flowers in August; Gold Haze, white flowered with golden-yellow foliage; and Hirsuta Typica with grey foliage.

Hebe (the shrubby forms of Veronica). There is some really good stuff for the small garden here, when you have sorted it from the dross. Hebes are notably good seaside plants, but many of those you see in our coastal resorts are drab and dreary, with white or washy mauve flowers.

Some of the more exciting varieties are none too hardy, but it is so easy to root a sprig, culled in autumn, in a glass of water on a windowsill (*see* Chapter V, p. 43) that by taking this simple precaution you need never feel bad about losing an old plant. The youngsters will grow 1½–2 ft in a season and flower the same year.

Taking this rather tender group first, they carry large spikes in bright colours and flower from July till December. The carmine Simon Deleaux is the most brilliant and exciting (height 3 ft), closely followed by the bright pink Gauntlettii (3 ft), while La Seduisante (4 ft) is rich purple with handsome, glossy purple-tinted foliage. In Andersonii Variegata (2–3 ft) we have one of the most telling, small, variegated shrubs with large cream-and-pale-green-streaked leaves, and spikes of deep lavender flowers.

An outstanding new hebe, hardier than the above, 3 ft tall with willow-like foliage, is Great Orme. Slenderly tapering, its 6 in. flower spikes open deep pink and fade attractively. Long season. Autumn Glory is a well-tried old favourite; small, purplish foliage and silvery buds opening to indigo-purple flowers in stumpy spikes. Seldom out of bloom. Rather sprawling habit, 18 in. tall by more across. Can be cut hard back in spring if it straggles, at the expense of that year's bloom.

Three of the largest growing hebes, 6 ft × 6 ft with very long, sweetly scented lavender spikes over a six-month season July–January, are Miss E. Fittall, Hidcote and Midsummer Beauty. All much alike and moderately hardy.

Some hebes look so like conifers, with tiny scale-leaves, that anyone not seeing their flowers could be deceived. Thus the hardy *H. cupressoides* can be grown as a formal specimen, to 4 ft, instead of a juniper. Matt green foliage with tiny white flowers. The shrub wafts a delicious aromatic fragrance. Grown entirely for its warm, yellow-green conifer-foliage is *H. salicornioides aurea* (Great Dixter Nurseries), 18 in. tall by 2–3 ft across, going well with heathers. Particularly cheerful-looking in winter.

Helianthemum. Sun Rose. Magnificent, densely mat-forming ground coverers for hot, arid positions. Like miniature cistuses but with a huge colour range. Single-flowered types most charming, but each morning's crop of new flowers shatters by 3 pm. Double-flowered varieties hold their petals for a couple of days and, as they do not set seed, their flowering season is months longer – June till autumn. Trim over after flowering or (with double varieties) in spring. Seed or half-ripe cuttings in July.

Many named varieties. Among the best are: Jubilee, clear yellow, double; Cerise Queen, cherry red, double; Wisley Primrose and Wisley Pink; Ben Afflick, orange; Red Orient, a magnificent colour but not so strong growing.

Helichrysum. Among this genus of everlastings with their papery daisy flowers, are a few good grey-leaved shrubs. *H. splendidum* (also listed as *alveolatum* and *trilineatum*) is out-standing. Stiff and compact, 2–3 ft; neat foliage and clusters of little yellow flowers at every season. Amazingly tough and hardy. Gets a bit shabby after four or five years and should then be cut hard back into old wood in spring. Half-ripe cuttings in cold, ventilated frame. *H. angustifolium*, the Curry Plant, has that smell when bruised but better, and similar, is *H. plicatum*. Silvery needle leaves on 18 in. shrub. Flowers profuse but undistinguished, at mid-summer. Yellow. Cut hard back afterwards.

Helleborus. Two shrubby members of the Christmas Rose tribe must not be omitted. Both are grand plants in shade and will make good ground cover in time, especially if allowed to self-sow, which they do freely. *H. foetidus*, our native Stinking Hellebore is not in the least objectionable, even when bruised. Very dark green leaves, split most beautifully into narrow fingers. Green bell-flowers edged maroon, in huge candelabras, December–April. *H. corsicus* has bold, trifoliate leaves, glaucous, edged with mock-spines. Green flowers, December–April. Both reach 2–3 ft with age and go well together.

Holly. *See* Ilex.

Hypericum. St John's Wort. *H. calycinum*, the old Rose of Sharon, denizen of dark, dank shrubberies, is still excellent ground cover in difficult places. Height 1½ ft. Should be cut to the ground each spring. Large yellow saucers, summer and autumn. Flowers best in sun. Division of suckers. *H. patulum* has given us the splendid variety Hidcote, with substantial golden-yellow flowers from late June till autumn. Six feet if unpruned, but 4 ft if shortened back hard each spring, which is best. Only semi-evergreen. Easy from cuttings or division.

Ilex. Holly. *See also* Chapter VIII. There are sixty or more named varieties of the common holly, *I. aquifolium*. Most are either male (non-berrying) or female (berrying). If a female is to carry berries, a male must be growing near by, for pollination. However, the compact *I. a. pyramidalis* is self fertile and free-berrying; it has a yellow fruiting form, *fructo-luteo* (Hillier). Both have the extra advantage of few or no prickles on their leaves. The most beautiful prickle-free holly is Golden King, with broad foliage, variegated gold and green. It is a female and would carry berries if grown near the male holly called Silver Queen (life is full of paradoxes), with green-and-white, prickly foliage. Half-ripe cuttings, July–August, but very slow.

Jerusalem Sage. *See* Phlomis.

Kalmia. Like many rhododendrons, to which they are related, kalmias require cool, acid-peaty conditions. Seed. Best known is *K. latifolia*, the Calico Bush, with clusters of bright pink flowers, crimped like the frill you used to see round rice pudding and baked custard dishes. June. Height 6–8 ft. *K. angustifolia*, 2 ft, suckering and slowly thicket-forming, goes well with heathers. Small pink or rosy-red flowers in June.

Lavandula. Lavender. Thrives best in full sun on light, well drained soil. On heavy, clay soils, the dwarfer, brightly coloured varieties, in particular, are apt to be killed in winter. If whole branches die, this is often due to the fungus disease, Shab, and the affected parts must be cut out. For hedging, 18 in. apart is close enough for dwarf varieties, 2 ft for the large. Trim over with shears in early spring, almost back to the base of where the previous season's shoots started. It is not worth struggling to keep bushes which have become old, leggy, and misshapen. Cuttings root so easily in a cold frame at any season. Seed is a good though slower method, but seedlings will be of varying vigour.

Old English Lavender is *L. spica*. Grey foliage, washy mauve flowers. Height 3–4 ft, July/September flowering. The most familiar named varieties are derived from this. *Nana compacta*, called French Lavender, gave rise to the darker Munstead Dwarf. Other good deep, dwarf (18 in.) kinds are Hidcote and Twickel Purple. These all have one big flowering in July with very little later. Avoid anything that calls itself Pink or *rosea*; a really filthy off-mauve.

The species *L. stoechas* makes a change. Main flowering season, May. Square-headed with a row of purple flowers on each corner and a top-knot of purple bracts. Height 1½–2 ft; space at 1½ ft. Some strains of this are hardier than others.

Lupinus. Lupin. The tree lupin, *L. arboreus*, grows in two years from seed, 5 ft by 6 ft across. Pretty, fresh green foliage. A huge cloud of sulphur yellow or white flower spikes, May/June. Sweetly scented. Dead-head and trim over rather severely afterwards. Old plants get broken up by the wind. Short-lived but easily replaced; really beautiful stop-gaps.

Mahonia. Separated from Berberis on account of its (large) pinnate leaves. Most popular is *M. japonica*, once called *M. bealei*. The real *M. bealei*, believe it or not, was once called *M. japonica*. Seeing is believing and the one to go for (the present *M. japonica*) has much the longer flower strands. A leggy shrub to 6 or 8 ft, with coarse, matt-green foliage. Can be kept compact by cutting over-long, woody growths hard back in early spring. Clusters of long, elegant, pale yellow flower spikes, strongly lily-of-the-valley-scented, from autumn till March. Dislikes full sun. Propagate from half-ripe, nodal cuttings of the large, rosette-like young, terminal growths, singly in $3\frac{1}{2}$-in. pots. July–August. Shorten the leaves by two thirds.

M. aquifolium is a scrubby, suckering shrub, but its variety *undulata* is compact to 6 ft or more. Can be pruned after flowering. Handsome, glossy, wavy-margined foliage, coppery when young, bronzy purple in winter. Bright yellow, honey-scented flowers in dense clusters, April. Cuttings as above.

Mexican Orange. *See* Choisya.

Myrtus. Myrtle. The common myrtle, *M. communis* is well worth the warmest spot, against a south wall, in your garden. It may get cut back in hard winters, but we have never lost ours in forty years. Aromatic foliage. Flowers similarly but more ethereally scented, creamy white with masses of stamens, in great profusion August/September followed, in good seasons, by handsome brown-black berries. Height 4–12 ft, all according to your climate. Seed or half-ripe cuttings, July/August.

Olearia. The Australasian daisy bushes, with a singular range of leaf form. Avoid the hardiest, *O. haastii*, at all costs; a dreary thing. *O. macrodonta*, with 3-in. long, holly-like yet soft, grey-green foliage, is nice. Domed heads of white daisy-flowers, June/July. Excellent seaside shrub, growing 10–15 ft high there, but can be cut quite hard back, immediately after flowering. Only 4–5 ft inland. Not for very cold gardens. *O. gunniana (stellulata)* is so thickly covered with its $\frac{3}{4}$-in. wide, pure white daisies, May–June, that not one of its small, dark green leaves remains visible. Height 2–3 ft.

Osmanthus delavayi is a winner; I have it at the four corners of a semi-formal sunken garden. Leaves smallish, rounded with toothed margins, dark green and glossy. Tubular white flowers, $\frac{1}{2}$ in. long in axillary clusters, all along the previous year's young shoots, April. The fragrance wafted by this shrub is like frangipani – exotic, swooning. Height 6 ft or more, inclined to get leggy. Can be kept compact and flowers more freely by trimming over annually, end of May, reducing all shoots by three quarters. Full sun or half shade. Half-ripe cuttings, but very slow; mist propagation much quicker.

Osmarea. *O. burkwoodii*, a hybrid with the last as one parent. Very similar but with coarser, privet-like foliage. Tougher and more vigorous but not nearly so attractive. Same scent.

Periwinkle. *See* Vinca.

Pernettya mucronata provides the best of ground cover on *acid soils* in sunny positions. It has dense, neat, glossy foliage on a 3-ft, freely suckering shrub. Seed or division. The great attraction is in the large and handsome berries, $\frac{1}{2}$ in. across, shining like china-ware, and in shades from pure white through pink and coppery red to purple. Snag: the plants that bear berries are female. You must get a male to pollinate them. When ordering, specify that you want a male and see you get it. Nurseries can be too vague about this. Davis' Hybrids are a fine selection comprising many colours. Bell's Seedling also good. Thymifolia (from Hillier) is a small-leaved male.

Phlomis. The Jerusalem Sage, *P. fruticosa*, is ever-grey, with a slightly yellowish tinge. Height 4 ft × 6 ft wide, and pretty hardy, though liable to get cut back in bad winters. Hooded yellow flowers in whorls. June–July. After flowering, dead-head by cutting a whole cluster, including the central leafy shoot, at one snip. A likeable shrub, this; quick-growing, drought-tolerant and sun-loving. Half-ripe cuttings, July. Not a real sage and no use for cooking.

Pieris. Very handsome shrubs related to rhododendrons and heaths, and enjoying the same acid soil conditions with a cool, peaty root run. The flowers of all are white, bell-heather-shaped, but in clustered racemes. Propagate by layers or half-ripe cuttings in August. The easiest is *P. floribunda*, a dense shrub with small, dark, leathery, laurel-shaped foliage. Usually 3–4 ft tall and can be grown fully exposed to the sun. I have seen a most effective hedge of it at Wageningen, in Holland. Upright flower clusters in April; very free.

P. japonica, 8–10 ft tall, needs overhead shelter or its flowers, carried in beautiful long, drooping strands, get frost-damaged. They come February–April and are larger than the last, as is the foliage. The pretty variegated form, with white leaf margins, is slower growing.

P. forrestii (*P. formosa forrestii*) grows 8 ft tall and likewise needs overhead tree-protection, against both frost and sun. The young foliage is brilliant lobster red and expands at the same time as the white flowers open – a stunning contrast. Direct sunlight scorches the tender young leaves to a frazzle.

Piptanthus. Once considered tender, and a wall shrub only, *P. laburnifolius* (*nepalensis*) now seems, after its 1963 ordeal, to have proved its complete hardiness in perfectly open positions. Fast growing, to 8 ft. Young stems blue-green, bamboo-like. Large trifoliate leaves, becoming tatty late winter. Short racemes of substantial yellow pea-flowers, about twice the size of a laburnum's, carried for six weeks, April–June. Very nice indeed. Easy from seed.

Pyracantha. "Fire Thorn." Commonly planted in small gardens but not altogether suitable. Most popular as wall shrubs, for which purpose the clusters of large scarlet fruits in *P. coccinea lalandii* can be spectacular. Any aspect, including cold north, and reaching up to 20 or 30 ft. However, once the shrub has covered its allotted space, it begins to thicken up and then has to be clipped back, which means that you lose a large part of the fruit.

Furthermore, the fruit suffers from the same scab disease as apples and pears, and needs the same lime-sulphur or captan sprays before and after flowering in spring. Birds will gobble up the berries in a matter of days. Huge flocks of sparrows love to roost in a wall pyracantha snuggery in winter, making an insufferable din, especially at dawn and dusk, and covering the foliage with their droppings. At its best, moreover, pyracantha foliage is sombre and depressing.

Used for hedging, in the garden, pyracanthas again tend to lose much of their attraction through clipping. A free growing specimen, if a space 12 ft × 12 ft can be spared, is a marvellous sight. Choose either the graceful *P. rogersiana*, a foam of white blossom in June, followed by small fruits in huge crops, available in red, orange, and yellow-berried forms; or *P. atalantioides* (*gibbsii*), more vigorous, very free flowering and with persisting red fruits which birds seldom fancy. Half-ripe cuttings, August.

Rock Rose. *See* Cistus.

Rose of Sharon. See *Hypericum calycinum*.

Rosmarinus. Rosemary. Always popular on account of the harmless little fable that in homes where rosemary flourishes the woman wears the trousers. The common rosemary, *R. officinalis*, is a sprawling shrub, 4 ft high, becoming gnarled with age. Never looks better than planted on top of a retaining wall and allowed to cascade down its face. Likes sharp drainage. Usually hardy, but widespread losses in 1963. The variety *angustifolius* Benenden Blue is more attractive, with fine, dark green foliage and rich blue flowers in May instead of the usual washed-out mauve. Not quite so hardy, especially when young, so plant in spring. Half-ripe cuttings, June–August.

Ruta graveolens. Rue. A low, rather dumpy shrub, 1–1½ ft, with charmingly divided, glaucous foliage. Jackman's Blue Rue has particularly good colouring while the green-and-white, variegated rue is especially delightful in spring. Leaf-smell pungent, when bruised. Greeny-yellow, star-shaped flowers in late summer, on unpruned bushes. To keep neat, cut hard back in spring. But I compromise by pruning every other spring, so that in alternate years I enjoy the flowers. Soft cuttings with a heel, May, in a ventilated cold frame.

Salvia. The Common Sage, *S. officinalis*, is the only really hardy species. One strain seldom flowers, but even if you want it mainly for cooking you might just as well get a free-flowering strain with masses of purple spikes at midsummer. The purple sage, *purpurascens*, has colourful foliage and eats well, as also does *tricolor*, variegated in several shades of green, cream, purple, and pink. Cut back after flowering. Height 2 ft. Cuttings, any season, in a cold frame.

Santolina. Low-growing, aromatic Mediterranean shrubs. Best known in *S. incana* (*chamaecyparissus*), popularly called Cotton Lavender or Lavender Cotton. Dense, neat, grey foliage. Undistinguished yellow button-flowers. Cut hard back each spring to keep neat and prevent flowering. 18 in.–2 ft. *Nana* is dwarfer, good for edges. *S. neapolitana* has the same colouring and pleasant aroma as the last but is more sprawling, with longer, more deeply toothed double-comb-leaves. Cut hard each spring. *S. virens* (*viridis*) is a neat, compact little shrub to 18 in., with bright green, vile-smelling foliage, and pretty sulphur-yellow buttons on long stems, June–July. Cut back rather hard after flowering. I have been unable to trace the parentage of a santolina listed as *sulphurea*, with foliage between green and grey; pretty, pale creamy-yellow flower heads and a neat habit, fitting it to be an edger. All come easily from cuttings taken at any season in a cold frame.

Sarcococca. Ground coverers that are valuable for shady situations on any soil. Flowers white, inconspicuous but welcome for coming in winter and for their sweet scent. Tallest, to 3 ft or more is *S. hookeriana*, with 3-in. willow-like leaves. Flowers autumn onwards. *S. ruscifolia* has glossy green foliage 2 in. long, on a 2–3-ft shrub. Flowers December/March. With the same flowering season and particularly fragrant is the 1–1½-ft *S. humilis*. All spread by suckers and can be divided.

Senecio comprises some 1,300 species, including groundsel. Only two need detain us. First *S. laxifolius*, often, but wrongly, called *S. greyi*, which is a different thing and not so hardy. *S. laxifolius* grows 3–4 ft tall by 6 ft across. Clothed with elliptical leaves, olive green above, white beneath. A valuable and quick-growing evergrey shrub for any open situation, especially the seaside. Straggles after a time and can be cut hard back into old wood in spring. Covered profusely, though briefly, with cheerful yellow daisies in June. Dead-head by cutting back whole trusses, including the central leading shoot. This is quick and helps keep the shrub neat. Cuttings at any season.

S. cineraria (*Cineraria maritima*), a dwarf shrub for the front of mixed borders, is possibly the best of all hardy grey-foliaged plants. Best either in the named form Ramparts, with deeply incised leaves, or White Diamond, with leaves not so finely cut but dead white. Should be pruned hard annually, March–April, to keep neat and prevent the appearance of its cheap little ragwort daisies. Height 2 ft. Soft cuttings with a heel in May.

Skimmia. The shining red berries of *S. japonica* are twice the size of a holly's, are borne in showy clusters, colour up in September and hang on, disregarded by birds, till June, dropping off at last from sheer exhaustion. But this is a female plant and must have a male pollinator. The small, off-white flowers, March–April, of both males and females (but twice as numerous on male bushes) are deliciously fragrant, the scent being airborne.

In the male skimmia called *S. reevesiana rubella*, the leaf margins and stalks and the trusses of flower buds, before they open, are a warm pinkish russet – very pretty. There is also, reputedly, a skimmia with both sexes on the same bush, which would be ideal, but wherever I have examined plants of this, *S. foremanii* by name, they have turned out to be females.

My advice is to buy one plant of *S. reevesiana rubella* and to let this pollinate one or more female *S. japonica*, planted 3–4 ft apart. The leaves are laurel-like and the height of the shrubs varies from 3 ft in a sunny position to 6 ft or more in shade. Leaves aromatic when crushed. Half-ripe cuttings July–August.

Spindle. *See* Euonymus.

Spurge. *See* Euphorbia.

Sun Rose. *See* Helianthemum.

Ulex. Gorse. The double gorse, *U. europeus plenus* is a fine sight in spring when grown in full sun on a light, impoverished soil in rural surroundings. Solid with coconut-scented

Chamaecyparis lawsoniana fletcherii

Rhododendron fastuosum plenum

Lupinus arboreus. Tree lupin

Skimmia japonica. Male plant

Pieris japonica variegata

Genista lydia

blossom. Height 4–5 ft. Must never be shaded or fed. Half-ripe cuttings, July, but a painful operation best left to the nurseryman.

Veronica. *See* Hebe.

Viburnum. *See* Chapter XI.

Vinca. Periwinkle. All make dense ground cover and are tolerant of shade but flower more freely in sun. Most have blue flowers, in April. They spread by over-ground runners and are apt to choke their own graces by a too dense luxuriance. For best flowering, therefore, shave them back in early spring. Will flower on subsequent young shoots. Especially important on the Greater Periwinkle, *V. major*, of which the form variegated with pale yellow is very nice, especially in dark places.

Of the many forms of the Lesser Periwinkle, *V. minor*, an interesting and beautiful collection can be made. There is the golden variegated *aureo-variegata*. Bowles' Variety is deeper blue. Then there are a white, single and double purples, and a double blue. Division, layers, or cuttings, pushed in where they are to grow, at any season.

Yucca. This group always looks strangely foreign in British gardens, but is often welcomed for this very reason. Long, sword-like leaves arranged in a rosette, give the plant a formal appearance which can be useful. Large, loose spikes of waxy white bell-flowers in late summer. Very striking. Propagated from the small buds, called "toes", at the base of the crown and among the roots. Line out, April, in sandy soil.

The largest hardy yucca, to 6 ft, and developing a wrinkled trunk like an elephant's leg, is *Y. gloriosa*. Its stiff, spine-tipped leaves can be dangerous. Inclined to produce its flower spikes too late in autumn. *Y. recurvifolia* has soft, pliant foliage (height 4 ft) while the dwarf, stemless, 2-ft *Y. flaccida* and *Y. filamentosa* are quite harmless. The latter has a beautiful variegated form with green-and-yellow stripes. All will flower regularly on good soil in an open, sunny position. Dead leaves persist and should be pulled off.

CHAPTER XI

DECIDUOUS SHRUBS

THE VAST majority in this group are ultra-hardy. Their parents stem from climates similar to or colder than our own. Hydrangeas are one of the few exceptions. They can be a little ticklish; the lemon-scented verbena and most fuchsias also come to mind, though the latter are a good deal hardier than is generally supposed. The mere fact of a shrub or tree shedding its leaves in autumn is a sign that it is used to a sharp differentiation between summer and winter and is only too happy to take a long snooze in the latter season. A pity we can't do the same.

Acer. *See* Chapter VII.

Aesculus. The horse chestnuts, always easily recognized by their decoratively fingered leaves, are mostly large trees, but the Dwarf Buckeye, *A. parviflora*, is a mildly suckering shrub, eventually 10 ft high and a good background plant. It carries the characteristic white candles abundantly at a most welcome time in any shrub: August. Division.

Artemisia. Its several vernacular names of Southernwood, Old Man and Lad's Love testify to the popularity of the old cottage garden plant, *A. abrotanum*. It has lacy grey foliage, nicely aromatic, on a 3–4-ft shrub and is transformed from the usual disorderly mess to a comely dome if pruned hard back annually in early spring. Hardwood cuttings, stuck in where you finally want your plants.

Berberis. *See also* Chapter VIII and Chapter X. In addition to the evergreen sorts, there are two outstanding deciduous species. One is *B. thunbergii*, more often encountered in its purple-leaved form, *atropurpurea*. The flowers and scarlet berries are mildly effective, but the foliage is the thing, for it colours spectacularly red in autumn. As is often the way, the green-leaved type colours up even better than the purple; it has a pleasant dwarf form, *nana*, only 2 ft high, instead of the usual 5 ft.

B. thunbergii is spiny enough, but nowhere near so vicious as *B. wilsonae*. This has rather mingy yellow flowers but excellent autumn colouring combined with ropes of globular berries which are a glowing coral shade and translucent. Height 3 ft. A thicket of this shrub is truly arresting, both visually and tactically. Seed or, to be sure of your varieties, half-ripe cuttings.

Bladder Senna. *See* Colutea.

Bridal Wreath, Bridal Veil. *See* Spiraea.

Broom. *See* Cytisus, Genista, Spartium.

Buddleia. Shrubs of rapid growth and, often, of somewhat makeshift construction, but mixing in well with herbaceous plants and other shrubs. I do not consider the orange-yellow-pompon-flowered *B. globosa* (semi-evergreen) suitable for small gardens, since it does not flower well if pruned hard and, if not pruned, gets too big.

The other species which may be difficult to accommodate is *B. alternifolia*. It has small, willow-shaped leaves on thin wand-like shoots and these are wreathed along their entire length, in their second year, with ropes of mauve blossom, mid-June to mid-July, even more generously scented than other buddleias. Pruning consists of removing spent shoots that have flowered and any other unwanted branches, immediately after flowering. I remove about one-third of my bush annually, but even so, as a many-stemmed specimen it is enormous – 15 ft each way.

In a small garden, the way to grow it is as a standard. Allow only one stem to develop, removing all side shoots to a height of 5 ft, and stake it firmly. You will then have a standard of manageable size which makes an alluring specimen, as anyone who has seen the examples at Wisley will agree.

The common butterfly bush, which you see everywhere, is *B. davidii* (*variabilis*), growing up to 15 ft. Prune hard annually,

in early spring, to a pair of buds at the base of previous
season's shoots. Fromow's Purple and Île de France are rich
purple shades; Black Knight is sumptuous and dark but a
leggy shrub; Royal Red is not red at all, but red-flushed purple.
White Bouquet and White Profusion explain themselves. July–
August.

With same habit and flowering season, but only 8–10 ft
high is Lochinch. Substantial, rich lavender spikes and attractive woolly grey foliage. Glasnevin Blue (Treasures) has an
elegant habit and slender flower spikes. All are easily propagated from half-ripe or hardwood cuttings. Self sown seedlings
occur frequently (witness the way in which buddleias colonized
bombed sites in the war), but are scarcely ever as good as
their parents.

Californian Tree Poppy. *See* Romneya.

Caryopteris clandonensis is a 3–4 ft, grey-leaved,
aromatic shrub with terminal spikes of glorious blue flowers in
August. May get killed in bad winters; needs good drainage
and full sun. Looks nice with red fuchsias. Heavenly Blue is a
rather deeper shade; Ferndown, violet-blue, flowers September–October. Prune hard each April to a pair of buds at the
base of previous year's shoots. Soft cuttings, May, or hardwood, November.

The growth and flowering of caryopteris can be much spoilt
by Capsid bugs. These shy but active insects run out of
sight or drop to the ground the moment danger approaches.
They suck out the young foliage and growing tips leaving
pock-marked, distorted leaves. Spray with Lindex (Murphy).

Ceanothus. *See also* Chapter X. Deciduous ceanothus are
hardier than their evergreen cousins, but they never achieve
such pure, bright blues, while those, like Ceres, which are
described as pink are woefully muddy. All are good wall
shrubs, attaining 8 ft in such a position. Also useful in open
sites, 5 ft tall with a wider spread. Their tiny flowers are borne
in large trusses, June till autumn, with two flushes, usually.
Prune hard, early spring, to near the base of the previous
season's shoots. Soft cuttings with a heel, June, or hardwood
in cold frame, October. Young roots fleshy and fragile.

Best known is the vigorous, powder-blue Gloire de Versailles. But a richer colour is provided by the equally vigorous Topaz. Henri Desfosse and Indigo are even deeper and more telling shades but their growth is weaker.

Ceratostigma willmottianum is a hardy plumbago, valuable for its blue flowers late in the year. In cold winters it dies down to ground level, but in milder years grows to a 3-ft shrub. Mixes well with herbaceous plants or with fuchsias and shrubby potentillas. The clusters of pure mid-blue flowers bloom from August till frost, but start earlier if the previous year's wood was not winter-killed. Prune in spring when you can see how much is alive. Just tip the shoots, if alive and well, but cut to ground, if not. Division in spring or half-ripe cuttings. June–July.

Chaenomeles. This is the latest name for the race of Japanese quinces which are popularly referred to as "japonicas". As japonica simply means Japanese and is applied to many other shrubs such as Aucuba, Fatsia, Kerria, Pieris, and Skimmia, its use here on its own should be discouraged. But it is difficult to suggest a substitute when the botanists have so unhelpfully chopped and changed from *Pyrus* to *Cydonia* to *Chaenomeles lagenaria* and now to *Chaenomeles speciosa*. Well may the multitude groan.

The Japanese Quince has a dense and tangled habit, but may be kept compact without any loss of flower by continually spurring back young shoots to within half an inch of their base, whenever you happen to pass a growing bush with secateurs in hand. It tends to be shy flowering when young, and is always freest in the sunniest positions. Hence it is particularly successful against a south wall, and may start flowering in January here. Usually at its best in April. Heights are very variable, up to 10 or 15 ft but only 3 ft in some weak growing, large flowered forms.

There are many beautiful named varieties in shades of red, cerise, salmon-pink, pink-and-white (Apple Blossom *alias* Moerleisii), white (Nivalis), and double pink (Cameo and Falconet Charlot *alias* Rosea fl. pl.).

Rather smaller-flowered and of a lowish (4 ft) but widely spreading habit is the first-rate Simonii, with blood-red blossoms.

The true *Chaenomeles japonica*, which we knew as *C. maulei*, is a spiny, suckering shrub with more slender branches, usually 3 ft high but indefinitely spreading. The flowers are weakish-orange, but there are more positively coloured varieties, particularly *alpina*, a bold, brick red. Propagation: suckers or layers, in all cases. All have aromatic fruits which make good jelly.

Chimonanthus praecox (*C. fragrans*), the Winter Sweet, is one of our best-loved winter flowering shrubs, largely on account of its wonderful fragrance, which is both sweet and aromatic. Not for people with itchy feet, since young plants need six or seven years in which to grow before settling down to flowering.

The Winter Sweet grows vigorously to 10 ft or more, with rough-textured leaves, laurel-like but uglier. Not a shrub for a conspicuous position. Though perfectly hardy, it is often grown against a wall to protect the opening flowers from frost. These flowers are bell-shaped, the outer petals dingy yellow, the inner, maroon. The variety *luteus* is pale yellow throughout and a purer shade. Extended season from November to February, so that if one batch of flowers is frosted, others follow. Prune by shortening back the previous season's shoots immediately after flowering, but no pruning is actually essential. Seed or layers.

Colutea arborescens. Bladder Senna. Rather a weedy shrub but fast growing, to 8 ft, and popular with children on account of its large, inflated seed pods which burst with a gratifying pop when squeezed. Yellow pea-flowers over a long season. Succeeds in towns. Prune hard back, almost to the old wood each winter–spring. Seed.

CORNUS. The various members of the dogwood tribe do different things for us in the garden. We grow *C. alba* for its carmine coloured bark in winter. Always go for the best, when starting from scratch, and insist on *atrosanguinea*, the Weston-birt Variety (Jackman), which has the most brilliant red colouring. Its summer foliage is pretty dull, but there are good green-and-white (*variegata*) and yellow-and-white (Spaethii) variegated forms which also contribute reasonably bright-red winter stems.

You should plant a red-stemmed dogwood next to *C. stolonifera flaviramea* with vivid yellow bark. The contrast, in winter sunlight, is electrifying. Both species flourish in really wet, even waterlogged, places such as a boggy area near a pond.

Prune late March, just as the new leaves are breaking. Rather than cut the whole shrub back to a stump, which is rather weakening, cut alternate shoots hard back in alternate years. Hard pruning yields the best bark colouring. Height 6–8 ft. Propagate by hardwood cuttings.

The Cornel, *C. mas*, grows very large, 15 ft or more wide, and I would scarcely mention it here but for its February–March season, when it is covered with a fuzz of tiny yellow blossoms, slightly green-tinged, borne in clusters. Foliage dreadfully boring but, again, there are several variegated types: *aurea*, gold and green; *tricolor*, yellow and pink and green; *variegata*, margined white.

There is a remarkable group of "flowering" dogwoods in which a cluster of tiny, insignificant flowers is surrounded by four large petal-like bracts. Of these, *C. kousa* is perhaps the most reliable, once it gets going, though it has taken my specimen twelve years to settle down to flowering freely. These bracts, 1½ in. long, are pure white ageing pinkish, elegantly tapering, carried on the upper sides of the branches. May–June and long lasting. On old specimens, the flower-decked branches are arranged in ledge-like layers in an entrancing manner. Good autumn colouring on suitable soils. Height 20 ft × 15 ft wide but quite slow-growing. The variety *chinensis* has larger bracts, 2½ in. long and is readier to carry crops of its red, strawberry-like fruits, but tends not to flower so abundantly.

C. florida is white too, but its bracts are broad-ended; more interesting is its variety *rubra*, which can be a perfectly fabulous pink confection, but seldom gives of its best in this climate. Hardy, but prefers hotter summers in order to flower

well and late spring frosts often spoil its blossom, in May.
Autumn colouring.

All the above flowering types come from seed, when obtainable (Thompson & Morgan), or layers. None need pruning.

Corylopsis. The name means 'like hazel' and refers to the hazel-shaped foliage. One exceptionally lovely species, *C. pauciflora*, deserves a place in every garden where the soil is not too limy. It measures about 4 ft × 5 ft, with twiggy growth and flowers in short, pendant spikes of open-bell-shaped blossoms, soft primrose yellow, coming before the leaves in March. Nice for picking. Likes the protection of other shrubs or trees, both against scorching sun and in case of frosts while flowering. Suffers in a drought. No pruning. Layers, or half-ripe cuttings in July, but this is tricky.

Cotoneaster. *See also* Chapter VII and Chapter X. In my opinion *C. horizontalis* deserves to be every bit as popular as it in fact is. An excellent wall shrub (but not on red brick!) for any aspect, including north, its fish-bone-structured branches pressing themselves against the wall surface so that it reaches up to 8 ft, in time, without any support. It is equally good on the flat, spreading outwards rapidly, but reaching a height of 3 ft only; or growing out, like a bracket, from the top of a retaining wall. Its neat foliage starts unfolding in February and is shed only in December, colouring to bright carmine shades in striking contrast to the vivid scarlet of its massive crops of berries. Half-ripe cuttings or self-sown seedlings.

Currant, flowering. *See* Ribes.

CYTISUS constitutes the most important group of Brooms. Although their tiny leaves are deciduous, the shrubs' green stems give them an evergreen appearance, but many of them are no great shakes, structurally, as is often the way with fast-growing shrubs, which they certainly are. They like hot, sunny places and rather poor, droughty soil. They are usually planted from pots and must never be moved thereafter, for their deep, fang-like roots are sure to get damaged beyond repair. None can be expected to live more than seven or eight years. Standards, though charming, should be avoided; these have to be grafted on laburnum and are consequently disastrously short-lived.

The many beautiful hybrids largely derive from our native broom, *C. scoparius*. Unless very sheltered, they should be given stout stakes all their lives. They grow about 7 ft high and tend to get leggy, but it helps greatly to keep them compact by clipping over annually just after flowering—not into the older wood, but reducing the green shoots made the previous year by half.

A collection might include Burkwoodii, cerise and maroon (superseding Dorothy Walpole, of stiff habit and weak growing); Johnson's Crimson, smaller flowered than the others; Windlesham Ruby; Killiney Red; Lord Lambourne, crimson and cream; Enchantress, old rose; Diana, bright yellow and primrose; Goldfinch, purple, yellow, and red; Cornish Cream, cream and yellow; Moonlight (*alias* sulphureus and pallidus) sulphur yellow. These all usually flower mid-May to mid-June.

C. praecox starts flowering mid-April and is one of the few of the larger growing brooms with a really nice compact habit, looking comely at all seasons. Height 4 ft by 5–6 ft across. Small, pale yellow flowers with a rancid smell (not a bush to sit near). No one minds a broom's flowers being small if they make up for it in quantity, which this certainly does. Two new hybrids derived from it with the same good habit and small flowers but May flowering, are Hollandia, purplish red, 5 ft, and Zeelandia, lilac-pink, 4 ft.

The Portugal Broom, *C. multiflorus*, is better known as *C. albus*. Though leggy and 7 to 9 ft tall, it is charming with its masses of small white blossom, again in May. Of quite different flowering habit is *C. nigricans*. This blooms July/August with terminal spikes of yellow flowers on the young shoots. These should be pruned hard back to $\frac{1}{2}$ in. of the base, each spring. Height 4 ft. Can be good, but is sometimes disappointing.

Of the dwarfer brooms suitable for the front of a border, *C. kewensis* is my favourite. Only a foot tall but spreading indefinitely. Large, pale yellow flowers in May. Looks delightful near forget-me-nots. *C. beanii* is a much denser shrub, to 18 in., and a mass of bright yellow in May. *C. purpureus*, also 18 in. tall, has rather soft, flexible branches, with purplish-mauve flowers May–June; the shoots on which the flowers were borne should be cut right out immediately afterwards.

Cytisus species may be raised from seed, but the hybrids should be increased by half-ripe cuttings, June–August. They are a bit tricky, though mist propagation has eased the situation.

Daphne. *See also* Chapter X. Many daphnes are subject to a fungus disease which strips their leaves quite early in the growing season and is so weakening in its effect that the plants die. This is the mysterious malady that gardeners ascribe to an act of God or of the Devil. Two or three applications of a copper fungicide at fortnightly intervals in spring when the young foliage is expanding, should prevent the trouble. *D. mezereum* is both the best known and the most susceptible species; its bare twigs are wreathed in purplish mauve, heavily scented blossom in February/March. Berries red. *D. mezereum album* has white flowers followed by yellow berries and is taller, growing to 5 ft.

Propagation is by seed, but in many parts of the country greenfinches have taken to the regular habit of eating the berries (for their seeds, not for the pulp) when only half ripe. Bushes need to be carefully protected, for the finches are crazy about this delicacy, once they've discovered it.

D. 'Somerset', sometimes called *D. burkwoodii* 'Somerset', a 3 ft, domed bush, carries its clusters of pale pink blossom in May and they smell of pinks. Half-ripe cuttings, July.

Deutzia. Close relatives of Philadelphus, but seldom scented. Winter buds sometimes stripped by bullfinches. Flowers in spikelets in the axils of the leaves on the previous year's young shoots. Pruning, *see* Chapter IV.

Of the dwarfer varieties, one of the prettiest is the pure white *D. gracilis*, 3 ft and densely twiggy, a mass of starry blossoms in May. At the same flowering time we have the graceful *D. rosea carminea*, 3–4 ft, of loose habit, its branches arching outwards with the weight of its pretty pink blossom. Rather larger growing but equally graceful are *D. kalmiiflora*, purplish pink, and *D. elegantissima*, purplish-pink, both May–June flowering, and about 4 ft.

Of the large growing types, *D. pulchra* makes a shapely bush to 8 ft with white flowers in long, pendulous spikelets, May–June. Contraste, June–July, a graceful shrub, has flowers streaked pink and purplish pink while the petals are fringed. Half-ripe cuttings June–August or hardwood in the open, December, in all cases.

Diervilla. *See* Weigela.

Dogwood. *See* Cornus.

Euonymus. *See also* Chapter VIII and Chapter X. The Common Spindle, *E. europea*, is by no means to be despised as a garden plant. Pink-red, interestingly shaped fruits splitting to reveal brilliantly orange-coated seeds. Height 12 ft. Would be useful in the background to act as pollinator to (and to be pollinated by) the form called Red Cascade, which is the same only better. Can be grown as a standard. *E. sachalinensis (planipes)* has larger fruit, deep red, and its foliage changes to startling carmine. Height 8–10 ft. Seed (of species) or layers.

Exochorda racemosa (grandiflora) is one of the most beautiful of pure-white-flowered shrubs in May. Rather spreading bush to 8 ft high by more across. Flowers in upright racemes along the previous season's shoots. The globular buds give the shrub its name of Pearl Bush; they open into cherry-like flowers, $1\frac{1}{2}$ in. across. Prune by thinning out weak, spindly growths. Beware bullfinch damage in early spring and winter. Seed or layers.

Forsythia. The brightest of early-spring-flowering shrubs is also the greatest delicacy with bullfinches, which often strip all the flower buds off, even before Christmas. Country dwellers should think twice before planting, unless fully prepared to protect their bushes betimes with black cotton or with rayon 'scaraweb'.

The commonest forsythia in cultivation is *F. intermedia spectabilis*, but this should now be superseded by the variety (a sport from *spectabilis*) called Lynwood. The petals are broader and more prosperous looking, not emaciated and twisted. Large shrubs, 10 ft × 10 ft, the blossom borne very densely, March–April. Best pruned as little as possible. If cut about much, they run to leaf and soft, watery non-flowering shoots. The best way is to cut ends off the lowest branches, which have splayed out with age and are wearing out, and bring them indoors in the New Year to force into early bloom. This thinning is all that's required.

If you have not room for a large specimen, plant one of the dwarfer types. *F. ovata*, with pale yellow flowers, February/ March, grows to 4 ft only. Arnold Dwarf and Bronxensis are quite miniature, flowering at the usual time, bright yellow.

The forms of *F. suspensa* are the most graceful. In the variety *atrocaulis*, the stems are black, effectively offsetting the pale yellow blossom. Very lax habited are the varieties *sieboldii* and *decipiens*, admirably adapted for growing up walls of any aspect (including north) and of any height up to 30 ft. Also good for pergolas and to weave among the branches of trees.

Lovely though the forsythia is against the right background – say evergreen shrubs or a whitewashed wall or grey weatherboarding – you do want to be careful not to site it against red, yellow, or pinkish-red bricks; it also quarrels with the bright pink of peach and almond blossom. Half-ripe cuttings July– September or hardwood, October–December, in the open. Can also be layered.

FUCHSIA. *See also* Chapter VIII. Gardeners are slowly and belatedly waking up to the quite unlooked-for hardiness of many large-flowered fuchsias that we had previously thought of only as greenhouse pot-plants. In the garden they admittedly behave as herbaceous plants. Even if winter spares their old growth, it is best to cut it right down, late March, since stronger shoots come from below ground level. They flower from July till the frosts and flourish in wet chilly summers when other flowers go mouldy.

Feeding and watering are their two main requirements. They are both greedy and thirsty and do better on heavy, water-retentive soils than on light sands and chalks. Will flower well in sun and in shade. Old clumps tend to get choked with dead wood. They can be lifted, split up, and immediately replanted in April or May, as soon as signs of renewed growth appear.

New plants, bought in, will be planted out late May – never in autumn, as they must have time to get established before their first winter. They will have been greenhouse-grown and will hence need twigging against summer winds, but in subsequent years, no support is necessary. I never protect my fuchsias except by leaving their old top-growth. Many of us were jubilant at the survival rate after the 1963 winter. If doubtful, however, mound your clumps over in late autumn with grit or spent ashes. Deep planting, with the crown 3–4 in. below the surface, is another safeguard.

As to varieties, it is worth trying out almost any spare plants you may have, except for ultra-delicate Californian hybrids and a tropical type like *F. superba* 'Thalia'. Soft cuttings at any season from spring to autumn.

Of the small flowered, best-known, hardy types, *F. riccartonii*, red and purple, makes a marvellous hedge or single specimen to a height of 6 ft or more. If old wood is still alive in spring, prune back to 3 ft only. The same with *F. alba*, very pale pink with pale green foliage. It flowers much earlier if some old wood remains alive in spring. *F. gracilis* is boring, but its variegated form *versicolor* is one of the best of all garden plants. The leaf colouring constantly changes from pale ashen to pink and it is very free flowering, red and purple. Height 3–4 ft. Cut it to the ground in spring. Shoots that revert to pale green need yanking out as they appear.

Of large-flowered fuchsias one might include:

DWARFS

Height 1 ft. Tom Thumb, red and purple, very prolific. Princess Dollar, red and purple, very double and prolific. Alice Hofman pinky-red and white. Display, red, with nicely flared mauve skirt. Collingwood, pink with generously doubled white skirt.

WEEPING or SEMI-WEEPING

Suitable in tubs or on top of retaining walls. Marinka, red

self with sealing-wax gloss on sepals. The Doctor, pale pink and shrimp red; very long sepals. Lena, pale pink and double light purple; one of the best and good at the border front, being only semi-weeping, 2 ft tall. Avalanche, yellowish-green foliage; red and purple, only semi-weeping, 2 ft.

MEDIUM GROWERS

Height 2–3 ft. Chillerton Beauty, bushy and vigorous, pink and violet (Forget-me-Not is very similar). Mme. Cornelissen, red and white (with red veining); rather upright with good foliage. Phyllis, pinkish red, gleaming in the bud; rather inflated tube. Sunset, flesh and salmon, late flowering (August onwards). Uncle Charlie, the most eye-catching; red sepals, curling back; long mauve skirt with broadly interlocking folds.

Capsid bugs are a great pest on fuchsias. *See under* Caryopteris.

Genista. The second most important group of brooms (*see also* Cytisus, and for general and cultural remarks). All have yellow flowers. They are much longer-lived than Cytisus.

Starting with the tallest and working down: *G. aethnensis*, the Mount Etna broom, can be breath-taking. Large shrub or small tree to 15 ft, with down-drooping branch tips. When flowering, late June–July, nothing but blossom is visible and it looks like a golden fountain. Takes longer than most brooms to reach maturity but is also very long-lived. Excellent lawn specimen and also occupies little space among other shrubs since it casts the lightest shade and can be underplanted.

G. cinerea and *G. virgata* (the Madeira Broom) are bulky 10-ft shrubs of no special shape but quick maturing and very free and effective while in bloom, June–July.

G. hispanica, the Spanish Gorse, a dense, spiny shrub to 3 ft, looks dumpy on its own but quite nice as a low hedge. Smothered with blossom late May, but is soon over.

G. lydia is in every way a more delightful shrub, flowering for 3 to 4 weeks in June. Arching, sickle-like branchlets. Against a pillar or wall, may reach 4 or 5 ft, but only 2 ft high in the open. At its best when cascading over a retaining wall.

Wide spreading in time. Propagate the first four from seed, the last from half-ripe cuttings, August.

Guelder Rose. *See* Viburnum opulus.

Hamamelis. Witch-hazel. *H. mollis* is always rather expensive because scarce, and scarce because in great demand and also because all plants have to be grafted on seedlings of *H. virginiana. H. mollis* is the finest of winter-flowering shrubs. The leaves are hazel-shaped, rather dull, but the flowers are borne regularly from an early age, December–February, quite untouched by frost. Petals four, thread-like, bright yellow (or pale primrose in *pallida*). Wonderful scent when sprigs are brought indoors. Rather slow growing; makes 8 ft in 30 years. Should not be starved. Sunny site with evergreen background, for preference.

Hibiscus. There is one hardy species, *H. syriacus*, with a large number of cultivated varieties. They are excellent town shrubs (to 8 ft, and more spreading), benefiting from the extra heat. Apt to be disappointing in the country, especially double-flowered varieties, which go mouldy just as a large crop is coming into bloom. August/September flowering. Blue Bird is one of the most beautiful with hollyhock-like single flowers. Goes well with Hamabo, blush pink with crimson central blotch. No pruning. In France they often train them as standards and prune all shoots hard back in early spring, but this would make the flowering season too late in Britain. However, overlarge specimens can be cut hard, into old wood, late winter. Propagate by layers.

Honeysuckle. *See* Lonicera.

HYDRANGEA. *See also* Chapter XII. These are the most valuable flowering shrubs from July till autumn and there is a good range of types, each with a long flowering season. Some are particularly strong-growing in full sun by the sea. Others like shelter and half-shade. Frost is a great enemy; gardens situated in frost hollows need to choose their hydrangeas carefully. Varieties which flower most handsomely in pots in the house or conservatory are generally unsuited to garden conditions. Because gardeners tend to put a pot-hydrangea – a present from a friend, perhaps – out in the garden when it has finished flowering, they often end up with a plant which makes nothing but foliage thereafter.

Most hydrangeas flower along and on the tips of the shoots made in the previous year. If these get frosted or cut back in winter, there will be no flowering wood left for the coming summer. So (with the notable exception of *H. paniculata*) never prune your hydrangeas by shortening back of shoots and never prune during the growing season, or you will encourage production of lush, soft shoots which will not have time to ripen, and will certainly die in winter.

Pruning of old shrubs consists of removing spent, gnarled, old shoots to make room for thick, young, productive ones. This is done at the end of winter when, too, old flower heads are removed, these having served as some protection to dormant buds through the cold season.

The majority of hydrangeas one sees are in a half starved condition. They are very greedy, and should be given, at winter's end, a heavy surface mulch of compost, rotted dung, spent hops – anything bulky and organic of this sort – boosted with bone meal or hoof-and-horn. They are equally thirsty. The surface dressing of bulky matter helps to conserve moisture later on, but frequent and heavy waterings will also be appreciated. Hydrangeas never leave the beholder in any doubt when they're crying for a drink.

There are two main flower types. The Lacecaps, harking back to the wild hydrangea, are flat-headed, with an outer ring of large, sterile florets and an inner disc of small, fertile flowers. They are light and informal in appearance but also make a good show. The sorts that have domed, bun-shaped heads, in which nothing but large sterile florets is visible are known as the Hortensias. They give the greatest volume of colour.

Colour in hydrangeas is a confusing topic but important to understand. You cannot just go to the nurseryman and say, "I want a nice blue hydrangea", or, even more embarrassing for him, "I want a blue hydrangea like that one of yours. What do you call it?" – pointing to a specimen in his nursery. Its name is immaterial because hydrangeas of the same variety will carry pink, mauve, or blue flowers according to the soil they grow in. These colours are interchangeable and soil acidity is the controlling factor.

On very acid soils, these hydrangeas will naturally come blue – pale, or dark, according to variety. On only slightly acid soil they come purple or mauve – rather nasty, muddy shades, as a rule. On neutral and limy soils they come clean pinks and near-reds, again according to variety. White hydrangeas stay white, whatever the soil. Only on aging, their sterile florets may assume a reddish tint but this is by the way, and has nothing to do with soil acidity.

It is a pity perversely to insist on having blue hydrangeas, if on your soil, they naturally come pink. The pink and red shades are very pretty, if you avoid the palest, washed out kinds. If your hydrangeas already come bluish-mauve, without your assistance, then you can help them to come true blue without too much effort. Water them weekly throughout the growing season with ¼ oz aluminium sulphate to each gallon of water, and remember that the roots will extend underground as far as the outmost tips of the outer branches. If you are not thorough in reaching all the roots, parts of the hydrangea will remain mauve. In any case the change to blue will be slow and you must maintain your efforts through successive years.

Obviously your task is easiest where hydrangeas are being grown in tubs or large pots and you have complete access to and control of all the soil they are using. In this case, start off with an acid John Innes No. 3 potting compost in which flowers-of-sulphur have been substituted for chalk. Then water as above and remember never to use hard tap water.

If you have a hydrangea like Westfalen which looks its best when pure red, but has purplish tendencies, you can easily eliminate every trace of blue by adding a sprinkling of carbonate of lime (sometimes sold as garden lime) to the soil surface. This is the reverse process to "blueing", described above.

Hydrangeas on chalk or lime soils often suffer from chlorosis: i.e. a yellowing of the foliage, because they are unable to take up iron salts. These should be watered with Murphy's Iron

Sequestrene, following the maker's instructions on quantities. Iron is important to a hydrangea's good health, but it does *not* change the flower to blue, as we all supposed in our youth, when we were advised to ply them with rusty nails, old gramophone needles, etc. It is aluminium which makes this alteration.

All hydrangeas are easily propagated from soft tip cuttings of non-flowering shoots, any time from May to October.

HORTENSIAS (cultivated varieties of *H. macrophylla*)

For pale blue on very acid soils: Mme. Riverain, Mousseline, Vicomtesse de Vibraye. All tall. Avoid these on only mildly acid or neutral soils where their pale mauve or pink colouring looks washed out.

For deep blue: Maréchal Foch and Parsifal, of moderate growth (3 ft), preferring some shelter and shade; Goliath, vigorous and best given full exposure near the sea.

For deep pink: Altona (5 ft) with deckle-edge florets, which change to attractive green and red autumn tints; Europa (6 ft); Hamburg (4–5 ft) with very large heads, deckle-edged, but requiring shade and shelter.

Dwarf reds: Ami Pasquier, Hatfield Rose, Westfalen. Red colouring goes with dwarfness. There are no tall reds. These grow 2–3 ft and need shelter from cutting winds.

White: Mme E. Mouillière. Vigorous and easy. 5–6 ft.

LACECAPS (cultivated varieties of *H. macrophylla*, *H. serrata*, and *H. acuminata*)

Blue Bird (3 ft) is charmingly petite. Blues readily, especially the central fertile florets. Likes some shade.

Grayswood, rather leggy in youth, 5–6 ft, requiring shelter and shade. The sterile florets open white and gradually age to ruby red. Long season.

Lanarth White. Pure white sterile florets, blue disc, pale green foliage. Best in full sun. Height 3 ft in most districts, but 6 ft and more in Devon, Cornwall, etc.

Veitchii, 5 ft, the best white lacecap in shade.

Bluewave. 5–6 ft. Very vigorous, more often pink than blue. Late flowering, August–October, free, bouncing, and showy.

OTHER HYDRANGEAS

Ultra-hardy is *H. paniculata*. Its variety *grandiflora* carries heavy conical heads of white sterile florets September, aging pinkish. May be pruned hard back annually, in winter, but nicest left unpruned, reaching 6–8 ft. *H. p. praecox* is lighter, more graceful with the sterile and fertile flowers mixed in equal proportions. July. Height 5–6 ft. No pruning. On good soil in full sun, another very hardy white is *H. arborescens grandiflora*, 3–4 ft with white bun-heads. Nice with plants such as herbaceous phloxes. July–August. Can be pruned by shortening shoots back.

Most thrilling of all hydrangeas is the species *H. villosa*, if you get it in a good colour strain (H. Davenport Jones). A lacecap with blue disc surrounded by rosy-lilac sterile florets; coloured thus on any soil and does not resent chalk. Vigorous; 7 ft × 8 ft but worth the space. August–September. Leaves rough and furry. Some shelter is needed. Good near a north wall.

Indigofera. Much hardier than realized, even unprotected, is *I. gerardiana*, a most attractive shrub of open habit with graceful, pinnate foliage. It bears a succession, all up the young stems, of rosy-purple spikelets of small but charming pea-flowers. July onwards. Prune hard back to near base of previous season's shoots, April. Height 3–4 ft. May get killed to the ground after a hard winter (though this has never happened to mine *) but throws up strongly from the base. Seed.

'Japonica.' *See* Chaenomeles.

Kerria japonica. 'Jew's Mallow.' A popular and indeed common, and very easy green-stemmed shrub with crocus-yellow flowers in April–May. It bleaches in sunlight and is excellent in shade, thriving on wet, stodgy fare. Looks delightful associated with Munstead Polyanthus (yellow and white strain). The best known is the double-pompon, *flore pleno*, usually seen growing leggy and gawky to 8 ft, often tied to a wall for support. Much nicer is the single type, with gracefully arching branches, 4–5 ft, garlanded with blossom like briar

* Nor to mine. – *Ed.*

roses. The dwarfer, variegated forms look diseased and often revert to plain green. Beware bullfinch damage to flower buds in winter. Prune by cutting right down to the ground all shoots that have flowered, late May (*see* Chapter IV). Division or suckers.

Kolkwitzia amabilis. This is a very beautiful shrub related to Weigela, but more graceful in habit. Masses of small, tubular pale pink flowers, yellow-throated, are borne on long, arching arms in May–June. Height 6–8 ft. Prune as for Weigela (*see* Chapter IV). Half-ripe cuttings, June–August.

Lavatera. The Tree Mallow, *L. olbia rosea*, is semi-evergreen but hideous in winter. Its dark green, rounded young foliage is handsome. Grows 5 ft in a season and carries its mallow-pink flowers continuously May–November. Marvellous stop-gap. Reduce shoots by half in autumn, to minimize wind damage, and hard back in early spring. Short-lived but easy from seed or half-ripe cuttings of side-shoots, summer–autumn. Some strains don't set seed.

Leycesteria formosa. A stiff, coarse shrub to 6 or 8 ft with green stems and hideously dull foliage. Pale, washy pink flowers with purplish-red bracts in drooping racemes. Purple fruits, popular with birds. I loathe this shrub, but many (especially flower arrangers) find it fascinating. Prune hard back each winter. Seeds itself all over the garden. You're welcome.

Lilac. *See* Syringa.

MAGNOLIA. Perhaps more glamorous than any other group of hardy shrubs and small trees. Their fleshy roots tend to rot if damaged. Never dig the ground near a magnolia. Apply surface mulches. They are quite greedy, and a large circle should be kept free of turf if a magnolia is grown as a lawn specimen. This grass-free area can be planted with windflowers, squills, grape hyacinths, winter aconites, etc. Ask for spring delivery of new purchases. Not always winter-hardy when freshly imported, as most are. No pruning needed.

The best sort for the small garden, with nice, twiggy, compact habit is *M. stellata*. It flowers when quite young in shell-pink blossoms fading to white, with numerous rather spidery petals. Flowers 3 in. across, opening in succession,

March–April. Height eventually 10 ft by more across, but
only after many years in the fattest of soils.

By far the loveliest white magnolia is *M. denudata* (*con-
spicua*) (Treseder, L. R. Russell, Reuthe). Of very pure
colour, its lemon-scented goblets eventually open flat, 5–6 in.
across, April. Delightful small, round-topped specimen tree,
12–15 ft high.

Most popular as a lawn specimen is the larger growing
hybrid, *M. soulangiana*; height 20 ft. Rather larger flowers,
thrilling in the mass, but with an indeterminate mauve-pink
flush which looks a little grubby. The handsomest of this clan
is *M. s. lennei*, with huge blossoms about the size and shape
of a 150-watt electric lamp bulb, rosy red outside, pale within.
It bears handsomely grotesque puce-purple seed-pods in
autumn, splitting to reveal shining red seeds. The flower
arranger's dream come true. I have never succeeded in germinating these seeds. This makes a large loose shrub, 12–15 ft,
good as a specimen or on a wall, where space permits.

More compact is *M. liliflora nigra* (*soulangiana nigra*), with
slender, lily-flowered-tulip-shaped flowers of a delicious
wine purple. It grows, slowly, to 8 ft. All the magnolias mentioned in this and the previous paragraphs flower April–
May, just before or just as the leaves unfold.

Of a different type, flowering with their leaves in May–
June and even later, are the very similar *M. sieboldii* (*parviflora*), 10 ft, and *M. wilsonii*, 15 ft or more, with nodding,
scented flowers, best admired from below. They are pure
white, bowl shaped, with a telling central eye of crimson
stamens.

The last two come readily from seed. Layers are the
amateur's best method of increase with the others.

Mallow, Tree. *See* Lavatera.

Mock Orange. *See* Philadelphus.

Paeonia. Paeony. The so-called Tree or Moutan paeonies
are only 3–5 ft shrubs, as a rule, but positively Edwardian in
their frilly opulence. They derive mainly from *P. suffruticosa*,
pale pinkish-white with a deep magenta blotch at the base of
each petal.

The hybrids and selected forms are in many shades: pale or deep yellow, pink, white, crimson, and red. The fully double varieties are so heavy-headed, even before a shower of rain, as scarcely to be practical. Each bloom requires individual support. They flower in May and June. Their outlandish Japanese (sometimes French) names are usually quite impossible. It is best to choose by eye. Ask for spring delivery; autumn planted specimens frequently never come to life. Their price is high enough without that.

The fungus called paeony botrytis is the bane of all paeony growers, and attacks herbaceous types as well. When their spring shoots are 6 in. long, it is a wise precaution to make a routine of spraying either with Bordeaux mixture or with any proprietary liquid copper fungicide.

Although Moutan paeonies are hardy, their other weakness is in making young growth too dangerously early and then getting it frosted. Hence a north aspect is suitable, its sunlessness retarding the paeony's spring growth. A tree paeony which has become unbearably leggy can be cut hard back into old wood or even to the base, in winter, and will break freely, but a year's blossom will be sacrificed. A better way is to spread the cutting back over two winters. They are very greedy. Propagation of this type is usually by grafting. Sometimes you can organize a layer.

Two smaller-flowered paeony species well deserve a place, in particular *P. lutea ludlowii* (*P. ludlowii*). Very handsome, pale green, deeply cut foliage, all summer. Clear yellow flowers, 4 in. across and well displayed, in May. Fast growing to 6 or 8 ft by more wide. *P. delavayi*, with blood-red flowers, 3 in. wide, May flowering and much the same habit though less vigorous, also has nice cut-leaves but unfortunately clings to them in the winter, when they are dead. Both come freely from seed.

Perovskia. Don't be put off by its name from growing *P. atriplicifolia*, sometimes called Russian Sage. It looks something between a sage and lavender, with grey, aromatic foliage and branching spikes of small blue flowers throughout late summer. Height 4 ft. Likes a hot, sunny place and goes well with all sorts of plants in mixed borders. There are two forms in cultivation and usually nothing in the catalogues to distinguish them. Avoid the lax-habited, suckering form and go for the stiff upright, non-suckering brand. Put a searching question to the nurseryman about this. Prune hard back to base of previous season's shoots each April. Soft cuttings, May, or hardwood in a frame in autumn.

Philadelphus. Mock Orange. Still popularly, though incorrectly, called "syringa", which is very confusing, since this name belongs properly and inevitably to the lilacs.

The philadelphus is a good white-flowered, scented shrub, flowering June–July. Foliage rather dull. If the leaves are stripped off a flowering branch, the pure white of the remaining blossom gives a beautiful spring-like, Japanese effect in the house.

The most old-fashioned and still the commonest philadelphus is *P. coronarius*, with smallish, rather dirty white flowers and the strongest scent of any. Should still be grown in its beautiful and less rampant variety *aureus*, which has golden foliage in spring, followed by plentiful blossom. Height 6 ft. Of the tall, 6–8 ft varieties with large single blossoms, you might pick Beauclerk or the compact Burfordensis, whose twiggy habit demands little or no pruning. Good double-flowered, large growing varieties are Virginal and Enchantment.

Of moderate height (5–6 ft) and rather spreading habit are the single-flowered types with a purplish stain at the base of the petals. Sybille is especially good in this group. Then there are some really quite dwarf kinds, only 3–5 ft high, especially well suited to small gardens. Such are Bouquet Blanc and Manteau d'Hermine, both with double flowers.

Pruning, *see* Chapter IV. Half-ripe cuttings, July–August or hardwood, November–December.

Potentilla. The shrubby potentillas are all forms of *P. fruticosa*, and have yellow or white flowers like miniature wild roses, with a tremendously long season, from May till November. They are compact bushes, very hardy and easy, and can form neat, low hedges. Occasional removal of old, weak

branches is all the pruning they require. Very easy from
half-ripe cuttings, June–August or layers.

There are many varieties, of which I would pick out Elizabeth, large primrose yellow. Its habit is prostrate at first, but
later it attains 2–3 ft. Donard Gem (from Slieve Donard), is
bright yellow, 3–4 ft. Mount Everest, white, 3–4 ft. The soft
orange-coloured Tangerine develops its best colouring in
shade.

Prunus. Besides the flowering cherries and other trees
mentioned in Chapter VII, this genus also provides some
little shrubs ideal for small gardens. One of these is the 4-ft
Russian Almond, *P. tenella*, which is wreathed from top to toe
with bright, yet soft pink blossom in April, before the leaves.
It gradually makes a thicket, by suckering, and is mercifully
always on its own roots. Very pretty with a groundwork of
double white arabis to show off the pink. Prune regularly by
cutting out about half the oldest flowering shoots immediately after flowering or (what I do) just before, bringing them
into the house to open there. Increase by division.

Another, *P. triloba*, is always grown in its double form
flore pleno. A shrubby peach, this is likewise garlanded with
blossom along the entire length of its previous season's shoots
in April. Height 4–5 ft. Commercially, it is always grafted,
so beware suckers. For increase, it can be layered. Prune by
cutting the entire shrub back to a stump immediately after
flowering.

Both the above suffer (except in the sulphur-laden atmosphere of heavy-industrial towns) from the fungus that causes
peach leaf curl. Spray, just as the flower buds begin to show
pink, with lime-sulphur or with a proprietary liquid copper
fungicide.

Quince, Japanese. *See* Chaenomeles.

Rhus. Sumach. There are two very distinct types here. The
first has compound pinnate leaves, like an ash, but larger.
It makes a big shrub or small tree, 12–15 ft, of rather grotesque and ugly outline, especially in winter, and is grown
for its brilliant (though brief) autumn colouring. Commonest
is *R. glabra*, but best is *R. typhina*, the Stag's Horn Sumach,

with leaves up to 2 ft long, scorching red in autumn. Its variety *laciniata* is even handsomer in leaf, being deeply cut, but colours less brilliantly to orange and yellow. All these sucker madly, and can be easily increased thereby.

The second, and far more attractive type, has simple, rounded leaves, is best on rather poor soil and makes an admirable lawn specimen. If it grows too rankly here, it is easy to let the turf encroach closer to the shrub and hence reduce its food supplies. Finest autumn colouring is attained from somewhat starved plants. My own favourite is the Wig Bush or Smoke Tree, *R. cotinus* (*Cotinus coggygria*), 8–10 ft high by as much wide. The green leaves turn to gorgeous yellows and reds in autumn. The shrub is adorned, in summer, with a haze of flesh pink, later changing to grey, composed of massed downy flower stalks and giving it its popular names. There are purple-leaved varieties of this; Notcutt's Variety, also known as Royal Purple, is deepest in colouring. Very effective all through the summer and may colour up reasonably well in autumn also. Best of all, in this group, for its fiery red autumn tints, is the green-leaved *R. cotinoides* (*Cotinus americanus*), but it must be starved, or else it grows hopelessly rank.

No regular pruning is needed but shoots can be reduced in April to keep the bush compact in its early years. Layers.

Ribes. The best known flowering currant, with drooping pink racemes in spring and a smell of tom-cats, is *R. sanguineum*. Sometimes grown near forsythia, with appallingly crude effect. Height 8–10 ft. Can be pruned back fairly hard immediately after flowering. Much less vigorous, 4–6 ft, are the deeper pink-red-coloured *splendens* and King Edward VII. The Golden Currant, *R. aureum*, carries its yellow flowers in the same way, but they are sweetly scented. Height 6–8 ft, April. Not tremendously showy but quietly pleasing.

R. speciosum, a prickly shrub, is nearer to the gooseberry. Quite hardy but ideally suited as a wall shrub. Fresh, tri-lobed foliage unfolding as early as February. Festoons of tubular, blood-red flowers with protruding stamens, hanging like fuchsia-blossom along the undersides of every branch in

April and May. Height 6–8 ft or more on a wall. Layers (Hillier, Reuthe).

Romneya. There are two species of the Californian Tree Poppy, *R. coulterii* and *R. trichocalyx*, of which the latter is to be preferred though hybrids between the two are also good. Leaves glaucous. Flowers 4–5 in. across, pure white with a handsome boss of yellow stamens. Good in a hot spot. Not 100 per cent hardy. Cut back to the ground in April. Height 5–7 ft. Spreads by suckers and can be increased from these, but not very easily. Hates disturbance.

Rosa. Roses require, and frequently get, a book to themselves. The most popular flower in Britain naturally has a vast amount to be said about it and C. E. Lucas Phillips has said it in his book in this series *Roses for Small Gardens*. With the limited space I have to devote to all the other kinds of shrubs and trees for small gardens, I cannot do better on the subject of roses than refer the reader to his book.

Rubus. Here belong the brambles and raspberries. They include some ornamentals but not for small gardens. Exceptionally, *R. tridel* 'Benenden' (better than the similar *R. deliciosus*) is too good to omit, though it grows 10 ft each way. Is quite unlike other rubuses. The foliage is currant-like. The 2½-in. white flowers, in May, resemble single roses, and are carried in great swags along the upper sides of the previous season's shoots, which are themselves often 10 ft long. Remove old flowering wood as soon as it has cropped. Hardy, but plants occasionally die suddenly, at any season, without any apparent cause. Easy from half-ripe cuttings.

Snowberry. *See* Symphoricarpos.

Spartium junceum. Spanish Broom. For other brooms, *see* Cytisus and Genista. *S. junceum* has hollow, rush-like stems which are terminated, from late June till September, with spikes of substantial yellow pea flowers with a deliciously warm, summery scent. Good for cutting. The shrub itself is gawky, to 9 ft, inclined to split in high winds. Most satisfactory on light sandy or chalk soils in full sun. Can then be trimmed over annually with shears, in March. On heavier soils, this does not work, as the resulting growth is soft and the flowers are attacked by the grey-mould fungus (*Botrytis cinerea*), quite spoiling the display. It is best, in this case, to leave shrubs unpruned and replace with young ones, from seed, every 6 or 7 years. Very fast growing.

Spindle Tree. *See* Euonymus.

Spiraea. Earliest to flower, March–April, is *S. thunbergii*, 4–5 ft, very twiggy and charming, a mass of white. Following it in April is *S. arguta*, called Bridal Wreath or Bridal Veil, the white blossom forming continuous bands along the previous year's shoots. Height 6–7 ft. These two should both be pruned immediately after flowering, when the leaves have barely started to expand, by shortening all their shoots (which have just flowered) back to ½ in. from the base. They get very scruffy if never pruned.

In May we have *S. vanhouttei*, 8–10 ft high, the blossom, again white, arranged in domed clusters along the branches. Also *S. prunifolia fl. pl.*, with neat double white rosettes in arching garlands. Height 4 ft × 6 ft across. This one's foliage has fine red autumn colouring. Pruning, *see* Chapter IV. Half-ripe cuttings, June–August.

The summer spiraeas flower on the current season's young shoots, July onwards. Richest in colouring is *S. japonica* 'Anthony Waterer'. The smoky purple buds open to rich carmine flowers in flat-headed corymbs. These go brown on fading, but if dead-headed just below each cluster, a second crop is borne in October. Prune in March by removing all tired old shoots completely and shortening the remainder by half. Height 4 ft. Old plants can be divided.

Sumach. *See* Rhus.

Symphoricarpos. None of these, even the dwarfer pink-fruited *S. orbiculatus* are worthy of the small garden. This entry is by way of warning, not of recommendation. The Snowberry, *S. albus* (*racemosus*), of dense Victorian shrubberies, is a fearful weed, suckering uncontrollably. If you must have it, for its pure white fruits, which look like moth balls, grow it in the sun. It fruits but sparingly in shade.

Syringa, as incorrectly used for the Mock Orange, *see* Philadelphus.

SYRINGA. Lilac. There are a great many more different kinds of extremely beautiful lilacs than is generally realized. The specialist firm for these is R. C. Notcutt. But while none of us would be without a lilac, we should not overdo them, for most grow very large and, except when actually in bloom (and quite often they flower only in alternate years), there is nothing worth looking at. A good plan, with a mature specimen, is to grow a clematis through its branches so as to extend its season of interest.

Lilacs are easily grown though greedy feeders. The sudden dying back of young branches, in spring, is more often due to a bacterial infection (blight disease) than to frost, and all affected parts must be cut out and burnt. Pruning consists merely of the occasional removal of shoots which are too weak to carry flowers. Always buy lilacs on their own roots if you can. Suckers will then be true to type and not too numerous. Varieties of the common lilac are not easy, though possible, to increase from very soft cuttings, taken late May. Otherwise layers. The rest are easy from half-ripe cuttings. Let us consider them in more detail in two main groups:

TYPICAL LILACS

Varieties of *S. vulgaris*. Avoid the pale 'yellow' variety called Primrose. Can look charming on the show bench, under canvas, which intensifies its yellowness, but in the garden is just a dirty white.

The best pure white single lilac (streets ahead of the common white wild kind) is Vestale. Maud Notcutt is also excellent. For a double white, the old late flowering Mme Lemoine is still unbeatable.

The same goes for the single, deep purple Souvenir de Louis Spaeth, most widely planted of all lilacs. Only a shade lighter, Massena is dramatic, with huge heads, bowed down by rain. Sensation looks like an old-fashioned print, each purple flower charmingly outlined in white. Esther Staley is outstanding in its near-pink colouring. For a double lilac-coloured lilac, I would choose Katherine Havemeyer, a good rich shade.

OTHER LILACS

The Rouen Lilac, *S. chinensis* is a hybrid you see a great deal, growing as large as they come, very bushy with slender foliage and great abundance of smallish blossom rather on the blue side, fragrant. Its parents are *S. vulgaris* and *S. persica*. The latter, in its white form *alba*, is one of the most delightful shrubs I know. Only 3–4 ft high with slender branches which arch over when weighted by its cascades of blossom.

A dwarf but stiff, dense shrub, 4 ft high by rather more across, clothed in neat, rounded foliage, is one usually listed as *S. palibiniana*, actually *microphylla*. It is smothered at the usual season with typical lilac-coloured blossoms, quite well scented, and sometimes flowers again in late summer. *S. microphylla superba (splendens)* is almost pink, very well scented, and always flowers twice. Small leaves and small trusses, but eventually grows to 8 ft, with a graceful habit. Makes a good hedge.

A particularly hardy race of lilacs, collectively called Prestoniae hybrids, has been developed in Canada. Large, vigorous shrubs with gracefully branching, pink-tinted panicles of blossom in May. Unfortunately they smell of privet – a sickly scent. Two good ones are Fountain (well named) and Bellicent (badly named).

Tamarix. Tamarisk. Although the fast-growing tamarisk could never be claimed as a shapely shrub, the light featheriness of its foliage is pleasing from spring to autumn and especially so when laden with dewdrops. There are two main groups. First, those that flower May–June on the previous year's shoots. These are represented by *T. tetrandra* and *T. parviflora*. It is difficult to keep these neat without losing blossom.

Far better is the second group, flowering July–September on the current season's shoots. Most showy of these is *T. pentandra* and its varieties Pink Cascade (Jackman) and *rubra*. They reach 12 ft if unpruned, but 6–8 ft if cut to the base of the previous season's growth in spring. From the young branches, every little sideshoot is wreathed from end to end with pink blossom.

Although they grow, by the sea, in almost pure sand, tamarisks like rather good soil in the garden and full sun. Hardwood cuttings, inserted direct into ground where the shrub is required.

VIBURNUM. A garden consisting of nothing but viburnums could still be a very interesting place. Among the deciduous types, *V. fragans* endears itself by flowering at odd times all through winter, with deliciously almond-scented blossom. Its clusters of pink buds open white on a 10–12-ft shrub. There is a good dwarf form, *compactum*. The trouble with this species sometimes is that it flowers most prolifically October–November, before the leaves have been shed. The stiffer growing *V. bodnantense* 'Dawn' is less inclined to do this; pinker in the bud, it is equally vigorous and, on the whole, preferable. Increase by layers.

The next group is spring-flowering (April–May) and the clustered blossoms are carnation-scented. The main parent, here, is *V. carlesii*, a stiff, slowish shrub, 4–5 ft high and a little wider. Very pretty as a standard. The pink flower buds open pure white, looking fresh and clean, but the foliage is dull and matt all summer.

V. carlcephalum has larger flowers (almost white even in bud) in huge clusters and makes a great show but is too coarse for my taste and its foliage is larger and duller. *V. juddii* is most markedly pink in the early stages; its habit is less stiff. This is good. *V. burkwoodii* grows to 10 ft in time and is quite graceful with polished leaves that often become scarlet before falling. The flowers are prolific, but not so clean and pure as with the others.

All this spring group may have their flower trusses eaten out by birds, when they look as though a blight had struck them. Half-ripe cuttings or layers.

Several May-flowering viburnums flower like a lacecap hydrangea with an outer ring of large, sterile white florets and an inner disc of small fertile flowers. Such is our native Guelder Rose, *V. opulus*. Well worth growing in its dwarf form, *compactum*, laden with shining, translucent red berries in early autumn. Foliage maple-like, changing to carmine on the right soils. Only 5–6 ft high. *V. opulus sterile* is probably the best known Snowball Tree, with a mass of sterile florets packed into a globe. Too large-growing for small gardens, 12–15 ft.

The best "snowball" viburnum, for any garden, is *V. tomentosum plicatum*. It grows slowly to 5 or 6 ft by 8 ft wide, with plain oval leaves, and its Snowballs are beautifully arranged on arching branches. Other forms of *V. tomentosum*, with lacecap blossom, are Mariesii and the very similar Lanarth Variety. Their branches stretch out horizontally, with their upturned flowers arranged in layers. Really delightful, but they grow into quite large shrubs of 12 ft each way. All the above layer well.

Weigela (Diervilla). Shrubs with masses of inch-long, funnel-shaped blossoms, often eaten out by bullfinches in the bud. Showy and easy but with mainly heavy and uninteresting foliage. Exceptionally, *W. florida variegata* is beautiful for six months. Packed with dark pink buds opening, in May, to pale pink, sweet-scented blossom, followed by cream-and-green-variegated foliage, which sometimes turns pink at the margins before being shed in early December. It is a twiggy shrub to 6 ft, requiring little or no pruning. For pruning of the others, *see* Chapter IV.

Very deep red with a long flowering season, May–August, is Eva Rathke, but it must be grown on rich soil. Less fussy is Bristol Ruby, with a terrific May–June display. Height 8 ft. Abel Carrière is a nice deep pink, 8–10 ft, May–June. Soft, half-ripe, or hardwood cuttings.

CHAPTER XII

CLIMBERS

IN THIS chapter we shall consider those shrubs which are adapted, either by twining stems, by tendrils or by self-clinging devices such as the ivy's aerial roots, to clamber their way through and over any obstacles they encounter. This does not include those shrubs which are commonly trained against walls, but have no natural climbing propensities.

Many a gardener finds that there are more beautiful climbers than ways of using them. His house has usually only four walls and the garage is quickly obliterated by one montana clematis. However, there are plenty of other possibilities. Mature and decaying trees and any large shrub (especially if it is rather a dull thing, like a lilac, in its off-season) can be used as natural supports. If you match the vigour of the climber to the vigour of its host, no great harm need be done by the one to the other.

You should generally not plant your climber right at the foot of a shrub or tree trunk. This is a dark, dry, root-crowded spot where the climber has little hope of getting established. Plant it in the open, in a well prepared, root-free spot, and lead it thence (with string) on to the outermost or lowest branches of its host.

All sorts of artificial supports can be made for climbers. Simplest is a pole sited, perhaps, as a vertical feature among lower growing shrubs or herbaceous plants. Or a tripod wigwam. Or, for heavy roses, for instance, a triangle of upright poles, held rigid by intertwining telephone wire. Then there is the pergola, usually spanning a paved walk. This feature does not have to be a continuous tunnel. It can be discontinuous, with the side pillars spaced from, say, 12 to 18 ft apart, and a simple cross-beam linking them, with longitudinal beams along the sides. In this way the climbers can get ample light from every side and can be admired from every angle.

On a building, most climbers will need some sort of framework to cling to. Wires can be stretched between staples or you can attach a wooden trellis to a wall. Nowadays the simplest answer is plastic square mesh netting such as Nettlon or the eight-inch Weldmesh. Both are light and flexible enough for one person to erect by himself.

Actinidia. These are foliage shrubs, of which much the prettiest is *A. kolomikta*. Its heart-shaped leaves are handsomely variegated, in spring, in green, white, and pink. Twining stems. Height 10–15 ft. Half-ripe cuttings.

Ampelopsis. *See* Parthenocissus.

Bignonia. *See* Campsis.

Campsis. On a sunny wall, *C. radicans* can be relied upon, in most years, to display its showy bunches of 3-in. long, brownish-orange trumpets, which bloom in late summer and autumn. Pretty pinnate foliage. Self-clinging. 30 ft. Increase by suckers or hardwood cuttings. *C. grandiflora* (*chinensis*) and Mme Galen are much more showy and dramatic but depend on a corking hot summer to do their stuff.

Celastrus orbiculatus (*articulatus*). An excellent twining climber for an old tree, with elegant branching sprays of yellow seed pods which split to reveal bright scarlet seeds. It should be picked in October for the house and will last all winter. The foliage turns pure yellow before falling. Always insist on the hermaphrodite form (from Jackman), so that you need only one plant and not two for cross-fertilization. Height 20–30 ft. Half-ripe cuttings, July–August.

CLEMATIS. In the wild, clematis like to fling their tresses over other shrubs and, although they can look well by themselves on a wall, their growth is better distributed when they can mingle with companions. They look particularly effective with climbing roses and, as the two both like rather rich soil, they can be planted within a few inches of each other. However, it is wise to give the rose a start of a year or two before planting its neighbour.

Clematis roots extend near the surface to a considerable distance, and a heavy annual surface mulch of farmyard or hop manure, compost or deep litter chicken, peat and bone meal – something of this sort – is the best treatment for established plants. The addition of chalk or lime when planting is quite unnecessary. They must be shaded at the root and they need plenty of water in the growing season. Hence, if you are planting one against a wall, bring it forward 15 in. or so, because the wall itself laps up so much moisture.

The species clematis and small-flowered hybrids have practically no troubles and are easy to establish, but the choice large-flowered hybrids are subject to a cursed murrain known as clematis wilt. Usually while in full growth, a young plant will suddenly collapse, having been attacked at ground level by a fungus. Yank out the affected shoot and it will very likely throw up a healthy young one after a time – sometimes after several months. But this too may contract the same trouble. Sometimes wilt finishes off a plant completely. We do at last know for certain that it is caused by a fungus which can exist in the soil around a clematis or on dead plant tissue. The best precaution, at present, is to spray the plant with Captan or Maneb or whatever you use on your roses against black spot, and use it every time you are also spraying against black spot during the growing season. Also, completely remove any wilted shoots. Deep planting, with about an inch of stem below the soil surface, usually ensures that a plant will spring to life again from the base, following an attack.

Pruning is a worry to the amateur. It can be considered under three headings.

(1) *Small-flowered clematis species*, and their varieties, flowering in April and May. These need no pruning. Such are *C. montana*, *C. chrysocoma*, *C. alpina*, and *C. macropetala*. If they become too large or tangled, after a number of years, they can be pruned quite severely into old wood immediately after flowering without any loss of blossom in the following season.

(2) *Large-flowered hybrids* whose season commences *before*

mid-June. These should have their tangle of growth sorted over in late winter, just as new shoots are becoming apparent. Cut out all the dead shoots and the dead tips of otherwise live shoots and spread out the remaining live material as best you can.

(3) *All late-flowering clematis;* those that start flowering *after* mid-June. These can be pruned as hard as you like, even back to within 6 in. of ground level, if space is limited. If required to cover a large area, shorten all growth back to 3–5 ft from base. This can be done as early as November or not till February, as you please.

For the amateur, clematis are most effectively propagated from layers, but it is no use layering shoots of the current season. Choose a woody piece of stem at least two years old. Soft or half-ripe cuttings of *C. montana, C. macropetala,* and *C. alpina* are easy; of the other sorts, not so easy.

By choosing your varieties, you can have plenty of clematis blossom from April to October, and most are as free flowering against a north wall as elsewhere. And they will thrive even within the full blast of sea winds.

Most vigorous and quick for forming a screen or to cover an eyesore is *C. montana* (white) and its pink form, *rubens;* these will rush up 30 ft into an old tree and are vanilla scented. May.

Next in vigour are *C. tangutica, C. orientalis, C. rehderiana, C. viticella,* and *C. flammula.* Up to 15 ft and all July–October flowering, with masses of small blossom. The first two are chrome yellow. Get Ludlow and Sheriff's form of orientalis under its collector's number, L & S 13342. The sepals are thick, like lemon peel. The straw-yellow bell-flowers of *C. rehderiana* are strongly cowslip scented, while the white *C. flammula* wafts a fragrance of Meadow Sweet. *C. viticella* has purple lanterns and the red form, *rubra* is even more sumptuous.

In early spring, the flowers of *C. macropetala* (rich lavender) are lantern-like and fully double, on a vigorous plant of 12–15 ft. *C. alpina* is much the same and charming in such forms as White Moth, Pamela Jackman (rich blue), and Columbine (sky blue).

The largest of the large-flowered hybrids start their season in mid-May, with blooms 7 to 9 in. across. The best of them flower a second time in August–September, but they are all good and I shall not go into details. Some have large double rosette flowers, 6 in. across.

Those like the famous purple Jackmanii, which flower on their young shoots from the end of June, have just the one protracted season of six to eight weeks. Their blooms are usually of medium size 4–6 in. across. The lilac-pink Mme Baron-Veillard is useful in starting its season mid-August and running on into October while the purple, cream-eyed Lady Betty Balfour is essentially September flowering. Tremendously vigorous and freest in a sunny spot.

Euonymus. *E. radicans see* Chapter X.

Hedera. Ivy. Only of recent years has the ivy come into its own, and this popularity has been achieved mainly as a house plant. But most of the varieties we grow in the house are, in fact, perfectly hardy. Ivies are as happy in sun as in shade, but are especially useful in shade because they will thrive where many other shrubs would not. They have two distinct garden roles: first, as self-clinging climbers and secondly as ground coverers. Many are variegated and these are especially valuable for lighting up dark places, whereas a uniformly green leaf can be a trifle dreary, in shadow.

The soft, cool colouring of the pale-leaved Glacier is just right on a hot-coloured brick wall. Bluish-green, variegated white, and small, neat foliage. *Angularis aurea* has a good gold-and-green leaf, while the uniformly coloured *Cristata* is quite a vivid shade of emerald, the leaf margins being crimped and mossy. *H. colchica dentato-variegata* is outstanding. The leaves are variable in shape and size, sometimes 7 in. long, and others quite small. The variegation of colour is equally irregular, in several shades of green and cream, some leaves being cream all over. A vigorous grower, mingling delightfully with periwinkles on the ground, or running up a wall at speed. Cuttings, any season.

Honeysuckle. *See* Lonicera.

Hydrangea. For shrubby types *see* Chapter XI. *H.*

petiolaris is another excellent self-clinging climber for a north wall and I have seen it coping with an oak tree, running up the trunk and then draping itself from the lower branches. But it is deciduous. Sometimes takes a few years to settle down and start climbing, but is then vigorous, to 50 ft. Flowers white, of lacecap type, June. Layers. *See also* the similar Schizophragma.

Ivy. *See* Hedera.

Jasminum. Jasmine. The indispensable, sweetly night-scented white jasmine, with clustered flowers, June–September, is *J. officinale*, a vigorous twiner. Its variety Affine has larger flowers but is too rampant for convenience in most small gardens. Where space permits, it mixes well with a montana clematis; they are well matched for vigour. The hybrid *J. stephanense* makes a change, carrying a great mass of scented, soft pink blossom, but for a comparatively short season, June–July. Height 15–20 ft. Half-ripe cuttings, July. Layers.

The popular yellow Winter Jasmine has no scent. It is not really a climber, so much as a scrambler. Looks well when filtering through another shrub, e.g. the woody stems of a wisteria. Good, also, on a north wall. Flowers October–March on wand-like shoots, nice for picking in bud. Keep from straggling by sheering back in April. Height 10 ft. Layers.

Lonicera. Honeysuckle. *See also* Chapter VIII.

First the scented honeysuckles. Our native woodbine has two good garden forms which give a spread of blossom from early May till autumn. The 'Early Dutch' Honeysuckle, *L. periclymenum belgica*, has heads of carmine pink blossom; followed in late June by the 'Late Dutch', *L. p. serotina*, deep reddish on the outside of the flowers. Both flower a second time, are shade tolerant and climb by twining, to 20 ft. *L. americana* (*grata*), July–August flowering, carries its blossoms not only in the typical terminal cluster, but in the leaf axils behind, forming graceful, foot-long sprays. A very charming pillar plant, in rose and yellow.

With a heavier, more cloying scent than these is the semi-evergreen *L. japonica* (purple and white) better known in its cream-and-white form *halliana*. The flowers are in pairs, not showy, but borne continuously from June to autumn. Very vigorous. May be cut hard back each spring. The variety *aureo-reticulata*, with a network of yellow veins, is pretty but shy flowering.

Now forget about scent and consider some honeysuckles that are grown for their visual gorgeousness. *L. brownii fuchsioides*, the Scarlet Trumpet Honeysuckle, carries clusters of moderate-sized flowers which really are brilliant and clear red. In *L. tellmanniana* they are larger, and a sumptuous apricot, flushed red in the bud; but even more thrilling than this, I think, is *L. tragophylla*, in which the bright yellow, clustered flowers are each 3–3½ in. long. All these are midsummer flowering. They grow best on north or other shaded walls. Propagate from hardwood cutting in a cold frame. October/ November.

Climbing honeysuckles (but not *L. japonica* types) are frequently ruined by an infestation of greenfly. Watch out for this and spray in good time with Abol X.

Parthenocissus. This is the name under which we now have to look for those plants we loosely term Virginia Creeper. Catalogues may also list them as Ampelopsis or Vitis. The coarsest, commonest, and most vigorous is *P. tricuspidata* (also known as *Ampelopsis veitchii* and *Vitis inconstans*). This is self-adhesive, with leaves usually 3-lobed but not deeply divided, and raucous magenta autumn colouring. Much prettier is the true Virginia Creeper, *P. quinquefolia* (*Ampelopsis quinquefolia*, *Vitis quinquefolia*), also self clinging, the leaves divided into five separate fingers, with crimson autumn colouring.

Most beautiful and refined in this self-adhering group is *P. henryana* (*Vitis henryana*), with leaves divided into 3 or 5 fingers, dark green with pale variegation along the veins if grown on a sunless wall, and magnificent autumn colouring on any aspect. Has to settle down before self-clinging strongly. Seed or soft, summer cuttings.

Polygonum. The 'Russian Vine' (it isn't a vine) *P. baldschuanicum* is just about *the* most rampant twiner there is.

Will cover a tree with ease. Foaming white, late summer and autumn. Can be controlled by hard pruning in spring. Hardwood cuttings.

Schizandra. A little known but fascinating twining climber, rapidly attaining 20 ft and happiest against a north wall (but not on chalk soils) is *S. rubriflora* (*S. grandiflora rubriflora* from Treseder and Hillier). Inch-wide, glowing crimson-red flowers, drooping from long red stalks, in May. Increase by its suckers.

Schizophragma integrifolia, a deciduous, self-clinging climber for a north wall, very similar to *Hydrangea petiolaris* but, I think, better. It has a flat-headed inflorescence and the actual flowers are tiny and inconspicuous, but each is subtended by one large, pure white, oval bract, up to $3\frac{1}{2}$ in. long and half as wide. July. Half-ripe cuttings, July, or layers. (Hillier).

Solanum crispum, the Chilean Potato Flower is aptly named, with huge mauve clusters on the young shoots in June. 10–15 ft. Prune hard in early spring. The Glasnevin variety (*autumnale*) is more intense in colouring and flowers over a long period. Soft or half-ripe cuttings.

Tecoma. *See* Campsis.

Virginia Creeper. *See* Parthenocissus.

Vitis. The Grape Vines. For decoration, the really splendid *V. coignetiae* is unbeatable. It will climb up a 60 ft tree and drape its long trails from the branch tips. Its enormous, lobed leaves, 8 in. across, change to glorious red autumn tints. Hardwood cuttings.

WISTERIA. These ultra-vigorous twiners will soar through the branches of tall trees; will clothe three sides of a house from one root or can even be trained, by continual spurring back of young shoots, as free-standing shrubs. All wisterias benefit from this spurring-back procedure, carried out throughout the growing season. It settles them down to the business of flowering freely. Only a few extension shoots need be left for covering the required area.

W. floribunda macrobotrys (long known as *W. multijuga*) carries enormous mauve racemes 3–4 ft long, and is the one to grow over pergolas or, ideally, on a framework overhanging water. On a wall face, its long tresses get hung up in their own branches. It is so vigorous that it needs, perhaps, six years or so of growing before settling down to flowering. Its white form *alba* is very pure, perhaps even lovelier, although its tresses are "only" 2 ft long.

But, for that swooning scent which, coming in May, seems to be summer's first authentic herald, you must turn to the more familiar *W. sinensis*. Its mauve blossoms hang in 8–12-in. racemes, usually with a small but welcome second crop in July–August. This is the best species on a wall but also triumphant in a tree.

Gardeners frequently complain of barren wisterias. This trouble can often be laid at the beaks of our feathered friends; in particular, house sparrows. Precaution: black cotton or scaraweb at leaf-fall, in December.

Increase by layers. If you find you have bought a wisteria with very inferior flowers, it is probably a seedling. Commercially they should always be grafted or layered.

SHRUBS AND TREES FOR IMPATIENT GARDENERS

Acer negundo variegatum, A. platanoides schwedlerii

Artemisia abrotanum (Old Man, Southernwood, Lads' Love)

Brooms (Cytisus, Genista, Spartium)

Buddleias

Chamaecyparis lawsoniana aurea Smithii, C. l. Stewartii

Cistus ('Rock Roses')

Colutea arborescens (Bladder Senna)

Cupressocyparis leylandii (Leyland's Cypress)

Cytisus albus, C. praecox and all the taller hybrids

Deutzias. The larger types

Escallonias

Eucalyptus (Gum trees)

Forsythias

Fuchsias

Genista virgata (Madeira Broom)

Hebe (Veronica) 'Hidcote', 'Midsummer Beauty', 'Miss Fittall'

Helianthemum 'Wisley Pink', 'Wisley Primrose', and others

Hypericum patulum 'Hidcote'

Lavatera olbia rosea (Tree Mallow)

Libocedrus decurrens (Incense Cedar)

Lupinus arboreus (Tree Lupin)

Olearia scilloniensis

Philadelphus. The larger types

Phlomis fruticosa (Jerusalem Sage)

Piptanthus laburnifolius (nepalensis)

Ribes sanguineum (Flowering Currant)

Robinia pseudacacia

Rubus tridel 'Benenden'

Senecio laxifolius

Spartium junceum (Spanish Broom)

Tamarix (Tamarisk)

Viburnum opulus sterile (Snowball Tree)

FASTIGIATE TREES AND SHRUBS FOR RESTRICTED SPACES

Chamaecyparis lawsoniana: aurea Smithii, Ellwoodii, Erecta viridis, Fletcheri, Fraseri, Stewartii, Wisselii

Chamaecyparis thyoides
Cupressus sempervirens stricta
Eucryphia 'Nymansay'
Fagus sylvatica fastigiata (Dawyk Beech)
Hebe (Veronica) cupressoides
Ilex aquifolium pyramidalis (Holly)
Juniperus chinensis, J. c. aurea, J. communis hibernica

Libocedrus decurrens (Incense Cedar)
Liquidambar styraciflua
Prunus hillierii 'Spire', P. serrulata 'Amanogawa'
Quercus robur fastigiata (Oak)
Sorbus aucuparia commixta (Rowan)
Taxus baccata fastigiata, T. b. standishii (Yew)

APPENDIX III

SOME NURSERIES

Wherever a plant mentioned in the text is likely to be a little difficult to locate, I have added, in brackets, the name of a nursery or nurseries listing it. Here follows a list of relevant nurseries and their addresses. It does not pretend to be comprehensive.

Slieve Donard Nursey, Newcastle, Co. Down, N. Ireland

Jack Drake, Inshriach Alpine Plant Nursery, Aviemore, Inverness-shire

Four Winds Nursery, Holt Pound, Wrecclesham, Farnham, Surrey

Hillier & Sons, Winchester

W. E. Th. Ingwersen, Birch Farm Nursery, Gravetye, East Grinstead, Sussex

George Jackman & Son, Woking, Surrey

H. Davenport Jones, Washfield Nurseries, Hawkhurst, Kent

Christopher Lloyd, Great Dixter Nurseries, Northiam, Sussex (Clematis)

C. J. Marchant, Keeper's Hill Nursery, Stapehill, Wimborne, Dorset

R. C. Notcutt, The Nursery, Woodbridge, Suffolk

G. Reuthe, Keston, Kent

L. R. Russell, London Road, Windlesham, Surrey

James Smith, Tansley, Matlock, Derbyshire

John Scott, The Royal Nurseries, Merriott, Somerset

Walter C. Slocock Ltd, Goldsworth Nurseries, Woking, Surrey
  (Rhododendrons)
The Sunningdale Nurseries, Windlesham, Surrey.
Thompson & Morgan, London Road, Ipswich (for seeds)
Treasures of Tenbury, Tenbury Wells, Worcs.
Treseders' Nurseries, Truro, Cornwall

GLOSSARY OF TECHNICAL
TERMS USED

anther. The part of the stamen containing the pollen grains.

axil. The junction of leaf and stem; **axillary**, arising therefrom.

bract. A modified leaf growing near the flower.

corymb. An inflorescence of stalked flowers springing from
  different levels but making a flat head.

dead-heading. The removal of spent flowers.

fastigiate. Of upright, columnar habit, occupying little lateral
  space.

filament. The stalk of the anther, the two together forming the
  stamen.

fl. pl. Short for *flore pleno*, meaning double-flowered.

genus. A group of species with common structural characters.
  The name of the genus is, in designating a plant, placed first
  and has a capital initial letter See *species* and *var*.

glaucous. Bluish.

inflorescence. Flowering branch, or portion of the stem above
  the last leaves, including its branches, bracts, and flowers.

node. A point on the stem where one or more leaves arise (*see*
  Fig. 7).

ovate. Broadest below the middle (of a leaf).

panicle. An axial flower stem along which the flowers are
  arranged on branching stalks.

pinnate. A leaf composed of more than three leaflets arranged
  in two rows along a common stalk.

prick-out. A first transplanting of seedlings, at even spacing,
  usually into pots or boxes.

raceme. An inflorescence in which the distinctly stalked flowers are arranged singly at intervals along a stem.

sepal. One of the parts forming the outside of the flower.

species. A group of individuals which have the same constant and distinctive characters. The name of the species is, in designating a plant, placed second after the genus, and has a small initial letter.

stamen. One of the male reproductive organs of the plant.

umbel. An inflorescence with stalked flowers arising from a single point.

var. Short for variety. A natural group within a species, occurring in the wild; normally given a name of Latin form, and placed next after the name of the species.

INDEX